# easy
# Baby Knits

## 50 Whimsical Projects for Babies & Toddlers

# easy Baby Knits

## 50 Whimsical Projects for Babies & Toddlers

Sixth&Spring Books
New York

**Sixth&Spring Books**
233 Spring Street
New York, NY 10013

Editor-in-Chief
**Trisha Malcolm**

Art Director
**Chi Ling Moy**

Book Editor
**Michelle Lo**

Manager, Book Division
**Theresa McKeon**

Copy Editor
**Daryl Brower**
**Jean Guirguis**

Yarn Editor
**Veronica Manno**

Technical Editors
**Carla Scott**
**Karen Greenwald**

Production Manager
**David Joinnides**

President and Publisher, Sixth&Spring Books
**Art Joinnides**


**Family Circle Magazine**

Editor-in-Chief
**Susan Kelliher Ungaro**

Executive Editor
**Barbara Winkler**

Creative Director
**Diane Lamphron**

Library of Congress Catalog-in-Publication Data

Easy baby knits : 50 whimsical projects for babies and toddlers.
     p.cm.
    At head of title: Family circle easy knitting
    ISBN 1-931543-26-7 (hardcover)
    ISBN 1-931543-73-9  (paperback)
    1. Knitting--Patterns.  2. Infant's clothing. 3. Infant's supplies I. Family circle easy knitting

TT825 .E2795 2003
746.43'20432--dc21

2002030408


Manufactured in China

# Table of Contents

# Sugar and Spice

Fashioning cozy comfy styles for your little one is as easy 1-2-3.

This precious layette set includes a delicate surplice-wrap shirt and matching bonnet with embroidered flowers, a ribbon-trimmed mock-cable undershirt and a textured hooded cardigan. A cuddly garter-stitched lamb makes a warm and wooly best friend. "Tiny Treasures" first appeared in the Spring/Summer '00 issue of *Family Circle Easy Knitting* magazine.

## MATERIALS

▓ *Marina* by Grignasco/JCA, 1³⁄₄oz/50g balls, each approx 195yd/180m (cotton)

*Bonnet*

   1 (1, 1, 2) balls in #001 white

▓ One pair each sizes 1 and 2 (2.25 and 2.5mm) needles OR SIZE TO OBTAIN GAUGE

▓ 31¹⁄₂"/80cm satin ribbon, ¹⁄₄"/6mm wide

▓ Stitch holder

*Surplice Wrap Shirt*

   3 (3, 4, 4) balls in #001 white

▓ One pair each size 2 ( 2.5mm) needles OR SIZE TO OBTAIN GAUGE

▓ Size B/1 (2mm) crochet hook

▓ 2yd/2m satin ribbon, ¹⁄₄"/6mm wide

*Lamb*

   1 ball in #001 white

▓ One pair each size 2 ( 2.5mm) needles OR SIZE TO OBTAIN GAUGE

▓ One set (4) size 2 (2.5mm) dpn

▓ Size B/1 (2mm) crochet hook

▓ Stitch marker, stuffing and one small button for nose

*Undershirt*

   2 (2, 2, 3) balls in #001 white

▓ One pair each size 2 and 3 ( 2.5mm and 3mm) needles OR SIZE TO OBTAIN GAUGE

▓ 1¹⁄₂yd/1.6m satin ribbon, ¹⁄₄"/6mm wide

*Hooded Cardigan*

   3 (4, 5, 6) balls in #001 white

▓ One pair each size 2 and 3 ( 2.5mm and 3mm) needles OR SIZE TO OBTAIN GAUGE

▓ Size 2 (2.5mm) circular needle, 24"/60cm long

▓ Five ¹⁄₂"/13mm buttons

## SIZES

All pieces sized for newborn (6, 12, 18) months. Shown in size newborn.

## BONNET

## GAUGE

30 sts and 44 rows to 4"/10cm over pat st using larger needles.
TAKE TIME TO CHECK YOUR GAUGE.

## PATTERN STITCH

Multiple of 9 plus 6 (12, 9, 6)
**Rows 1 and 13 (RS)** Purl.
**Rows 2 and 14** Knit
**Rows 3, 5, 9, 11, 15, 17, 21 and 23** Knit.
**Rows 4, 6, 8, 10, 12, 16, 18, 20 and 22** Purl.
**Row 7** K2 (0, 3, 2), k2tog, *yo, k7, k2tog; rep from *, end yo, k2 (1, 4, 2).
**Row 19** K3 (1, 4, 3) *k4, k2tog, yo, k3; rep from *, end last rep k6 (5, 8, 6).

**Row 24** Purl.
Rep rows 1-24 for pat st.

**Bonnet**
With smaller needles cast on 96 (102, 108, 114) sts. Work in St st for ³⁄₄"/2cm, end with a WS row. Change to larger needles. **Eyelet turning row (RS)** K1, *k2tog, yo; rep from * to last st, k1. Work in St st for ³⁄₄"/2cm. Work in pat st until piece measures 4³⁄₄ (5, 5¹⁄₄, 5¹⁄₂)"/12 (12.5, 13, 13.5)cm above eyelet row.

## Top shaping

Bind off 5 (5, 6, 7) sts at beg of next 8 (4, 4, 4) rows, 6 sts at beg of next 4 (8, 8, 8) rows—32 (34, 36, 38) sts. Dec 1 st each side [every 4th row once, every 5th row once] 4 (4, 4, 5) times, every 4th row 0 (1, 1, 0) time—16 (16, 18, 18) sts. Work even until piece measures 9½ (10, 10¼, 10½)"/24 (25, 26, 27)cm above eyelet row. Place sts on a holder.

FINISHING

Block piece. Fold in half and sew open sts tog for back seam. Fold at eyelet row to WS and sew hem in place.

### Lower edging

With RS facing and larger needles, pick up and k 74 (76, 80, 84) sts evenly along lower edge, including side of picot edge. Work in St st for ¾"/2cm. Work eyelet turning ridge as before. Change to smaller needles and work in St st for ¾"/2cm more. Bind off. Fold edging to WS at eyelet row and sew in place. Weave ribbon through center of band. Make two ¾"/2cm pompoms and sew to each end of ribbon. Embroider flowers using lazy daisy st (see photo for placement).

## SURPLICE WRAP SHIRT

### FINISHED MEASUREMENTS

■ Chest (closed) 22 (23½, 25, 27)"/56 (59.5, 63.5, 68.5)cm
■ Length 10¼ (11, 11¾, 12¾)"/26 (28, 30, 32)cm
■ Upper arm 10 (10½, 11½, 12¼)"/25.5 (27, 29, 31)cm

### GAUGE

30 sts and 44 rows to 4"/10cm over chart 1 using size 2 (2.5mm) needles.
TAKE TIME TO CHECK YOUR GAUGE.

### Note

Be sure that there is always a yo to compensate for each dec in every row to keep st count the same. If there is not, then omit the yo or dec and work in St st.

BACK

Cast on 82 (88, 94, 100) sts.

### Beg chart 1

**Row 1 (RS)** Beg with st 4 (1, 2, 4) work to st 12, work sts 4 to 12 (9-st rep) 8 (8, 9, 10) times, end with st 13 (16, 14, 13). Cont in pat as established until piece measures 5½ (6, 6¼, 6¾)"/14 (15, 16, 17)cm from beg, end with a WS row.

### Armhole shaping

Bind off 3 sts at beg of next 2 rows, 2 sts at beg of next 4 rows, dec 1 st each side every other row once—66 (72, 78, 84) sts. Work even until armhole measures 4¾ (5, 5½, 6)"/12 (13, 14, 15)cm. Bind off all sts.

LEFT FRONT

Cast on 70 (73, 76, 79) sts.

### Beg chart 1

**Row 1 (RS)** Beg with st 4 (1, 2, 4) work to st 12, work sts 4 to 12 (9-st rep) 6 (6, 7, 7) times, work sts 4 to 10 (10, 5, 10). Cont in pat as established until same length as back to armhole. Work armhole decs at beg of RS rows as for back—62 (65, 68, 71) sts. Work even until piece measures 7 (7½, 7¾, 8¼)"/18 (19, 20, 21)cm from beg, end with a RS row.

### Neck shaping

**Next row (WS)** Bind off 9 (10, 11, 12) sts (neck edge), work to end. Cont to bind off from neck edge 3 sts 3 times, 2 sts 10 times, 1 st 4 (5, 6, 7) times. Work even until same length as back. Bind off rem 20 (21, 22, 23) sts for shoulder.

RIGHT FRONT

Work to correspond to left front, reversing all shaping and work chart 1 as foll:
**Row 1 (RS)** Beg with st 7 (7, 11, 7) work to st 12, work sts 4 to 12 (9-st rep) 7 (7, 8, 8) times, end with st 13 (16, 14, 13).

SLEEVES

Cast on 38 (40, 44, 46) sts.

### Beg chart 2

**Row 1 (RS)** Beg with st 3 (2, 9, 8) work to st 12, work sts 4 to 12 (9-st rep) 3 (3, 4, 5) times, end with st 13 (14, 16, 8). Cont in pat as established, inc 1 st each side (working inc sts into chart pat) every 4th row 11 (13, 18, 19) times, every other row 7 (7, 3, 4) times—74 (80, 86, 92) sts. Work even until piece measures 6¼ (7, 8, 8½)"/16 (18, 20.5, 22)cm from beg, end with a WS row.

### Cap shaping

Bind off 7 sts at beg of next 2 rows, 5 sts at beg of next 2 rows, 4 sts at beg of next 4 rows, 6 sts at beg of next 4 rows. Bind off rem 10 (16, 22, 28) sts.

FINISHING

Block pieces to measurements. Sew shoulder seams. Set in sleeves. Sew side and sleeve seams.

### Picot edging

With RS facing and crochet hook, work around outside edge of jacket as foll:
**Rnd 1** Work sc evenly around, so that you have a multiple of 4 sts.
**Rnd 2** *Sc in each of next 3 sc, ch 3, sl st in first ch, skip 1 sc; rep from * around. Fasten off.
Work edging in same way around lower edge of sleeves.
Embroider flowers using lazy daisy st on fronts and back (see photo for placement). Cut ribbon into 3 equal lengths and attach to fronts for closures (see photo).

## LAMB

### GAUGE

30 sts and 40 rows to 4"/10cm over St st using size 2 (2.5mm) needles.
TAKE TIME TO CHECK YOUR GAUGE.

### TOP OF BODY

Cast on 22 sts. Work in garter st for 76 rows. Inc 1 st each side as foll: every 3rd row 23 times—68 sts. Bind off 2 sts at beg of next 2 rows, dec 1 st each side every other row twice. Bind off rem 60 sts.

## BOTTOM OF BODY

Cast on 14 sts. Work in St st for 114 rows. Inc 1 st each side every 14th row twice, every 8th row 4 times—26 sts. Dec 1 st each side every 8th row 4 times, every 4th row 4 times. Bind off rem 10 sts.

## PAWS

(make 4)

With dpn, cast on 21 sts. Divide sts evenly over 3 needles. Join, taking care not to twist sts on needles. Place marker for end of rnd and sl marker every rnd. Work in St st (k every rnd) for 34 rnds. Cut yarn. Draw through sts and pull tog tightly and secure. Stuff.

## HEAD

With dpn, cast on 50 sts. Divide sts and join as before. Work in rnds of garter st (k 1 rnd, p 1 rnd) for 34 rnds. Cont in St st for 17 rnds. [Dec 10 sts evenly on next rnd. K 1 rnd] 4 times—10 sts. Cut yarn. Draw through sts and pull tog tightly and secure. Stuff.

## EARS

(make 4)

Cast on 16 sts and work in St st for 4 rows. **Next (dec) row (RS)** K1, SKP, k to last 3 sts, k2tog, k1. Rep dec row every 4th row 3 times more, then every other row twice—4 sts. Cut yarn. Draw through sts and pull tog tightly and secure. With WS of two ears tog, sew side seams.

## FINISHING

Sew top and bottom of body tog, leaving a small opening. Stuff and sew opening closed. Embroider eyes on face with French knots. Sew on button for nose. Sew on legs and head. Sew on ears, gathering slightly at lower edge.

## TAIL

With crochet hook, ch 2"/5cm. Sc in each ch. Fasten off and attach to sheep.

## UNDERSHIRT

### FINISHED MEASUREMENTS

- Chest 19 (21, 22½, 24)"/48 (53, 57, 61)cm
- Length 12½ (13½, 14, 15)"/31.5 (34.5, 35.5, 38)cm

### GAUGE

31 sts and 44 rows to 4"/10cm over chart pat using larger needles.
TAKE TIME TO CHECK YOUR GAUGE.

### Note

**1** Be sure that there is always a yo to compensate for each dec in every row to keep st count the same. If there is not, then omit the yo or dec and work in St st.

**2** K first and last st of every row for selvage st.

### BACK

With smaller needles, cast on 75 (81, 87, 93) sts. Work in St st for 1¼"/3cm. **Eyelet turning row (RS)** K1, *k2tog, yo; rep from * to last 2 sts, k2. Work in St st for 1¼"/3cm more. Change to larger needles.

### Beg chart

**Row 1 (RS)** K1 (selvage st), beg with st 4 (1, 5, 2) work to st 18, work sts 5 to 18 (14-st rep) 4 (4, 5, 5) times, end with st 20 (23, 19, 22). Cont in pat as established until piece measures 6½ (7, 7½, 8)"/16.5 (18, 19, 20.5)cm above eyelet row, end with a WS row.

### Armhole shaping

Bind off 3 sts at beg of next 2 rows, 2 sts at beg of next 2 rows, dec 1 st each side every other row 4 times—57 (63, 69, 75) sts. Work even until armhole measures 4 (4½, 4½, 5)"/10 (11.5, 11.5, 12.5)cm.

### Neck shaping

**Next row (RS)** Work 16 sts, join 2nd ball of yarn and bind off center 25 (31, 37, 43) sts, work to end. Working both sides at once, bind off from each neck edge 3 sts once, 2 sts twice, 1 st 3 times, 2 sts 3 times. With RS facing and smaller needles, pick up and k sts evenly around neck edge. Work in St st for 3 rows. Work eyelet turning row as for back. Work in St st for 3 more rows. Bind off. Fold band in half to WS and sew in place.

## FRONT

Work as for back until armhole measures 3 (3½, 3½, 4)"/7.5 (9, 9, 10)cm.

### Neck shaping

**Next row (RS)** Work 24 sts, join 2nd ball of yarn and bind off center 9 (15, 21, 27) sts, work to end. Working both sides at once, bind off from each neck edge 3 sts once, 2 sts twice, 1 st 7 times, 2 sts 5 times. Work eyelet edging around neck as of back.

### FINISHING

Overlap back 2"/5cm over the front and sew in place. Work eyelet edging around each armhole as for neck. Weave ribbon through eyelet row at lower edge of body and tie sides (see photo).

## HOODED CARDIGAN

### FINISHED MEASUREMENTS

- Chest (buttoned) 20 (21¾, 23, 24¾)"/50.5 (55.5, 58.5, 63)cm
- Length 10¼ (11, 12, 13)"/26 (28.5, 30.5, 33)cm
- Upper arm 9½ (10¼, 10¾, 11½)"/24 (26, 27.5, 29)cm

### GAUGE

32 sts and 40 rows to 4"/10cm over chart pat using larger needles.
TAKE TIME TO CHECK YOUR GAUGE.

### BACK

With smaller needles, cast on 80 (86, 92, 98) sts. Work in k2, p2 rib for 4 rows. Change to larger needles.

### Beg chart

**Row 1 (RS)** Beg with st 21 (18, 3, 1) work to st 22, work sts 1 to 22 four times, end with st 12 (15, 6, 10). Cont in pat as established until piece measures 5½ (6, 6½, 7)"/14 (15.5, 16.5, 17.5)cm from beg, end with a WS row.

### Armhole shaping

Bind off 2 sts at beg of next 4 rows, dec 1 st each side every other row 3 times—66 (72, 78,

84) sts. Work even until armhole measures 4³⁄₄ (5, 5¹⁄₂, 6)"/12 (13, 14, 15)cm. Bind off all sts.

### LEFT FRONT

With smaller needles, cast on 39 (42, 45, 48) sts. Work in k2, p2 rib for 4 rows. Change to larger needles.

### Beg chart

**Row 1 (RS)** Beg with 21 (18, 3, 1) work to st 22, work sts 1 to 22 twice, end with st 15 (15, 3, 4). Cont in pat as established until same length as back to armhole. Work armhole decs at beg of RS rows as for back—32 (35, 38, 41) sts. Work even until piece measures 8³⁄₄ (9¹⁄₂, 10¹⁄₂, 11¹⁄₂)"/22 (24.5, 26.5, 29)cm from beg, end with a RS row.

### Neck shaping

**Next row (WS)** Bind off 3 (4, 5, 6) sts (neck edge), work to end. Cont to bind off from neck edge 2 sts 3 times, 1 st 3 times. Work even until same length as back. Bind off rem 20 (22, 24, 26) sts for shoulder.

### RIGHT FRONT

Work to correspond to left front, reversing all shaping and work chart as foll:

**Row 1 (RS)** Beg with st 18 (18, 6, 7) work to st 22, work sts 1 to 22 twice, end with st 12 (15, 6, 10).

### SLEEVES

With smaller needles, cast on 40 (42, 44, 46) sts. Work in k2, p2 rib for 4 rows. Change to larger needles.

### Beg chart

**Row 1 (RS)** Beg with st 19 (18, 17, 16) work to st 22, work sts 1 to 22 twice, end with st 14 (15, 16, 17). Cont in pat as established, inc 1 st each side (working inc sts into chart pat) every other row 11 (12, 9, 11) times, every 4th row 7 (8, 12, 12) times—76 (82, 86, 92) sts. Work even until piece measures 6¹⁄₂ (7, 8, 8¹⁄₂)"/16.5 (17.5, 20.5, 21.5)cm from beg, end with a WS row.

### Cap shaping

Bind off 2 sts at beg of next 2 rows, 3 sts at beg of next 2 rows, 4 sts at beg of next 4 rows, 5 sts at beg of next 2 rows, 6 sts at beg of next 2 rows. Bind off rem 28 (34, 38, 44) sts.

**SURPLICE WRAP SHIRT**

**UNDERSHIRT**

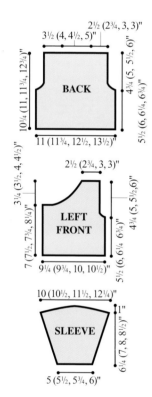

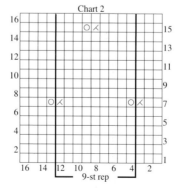

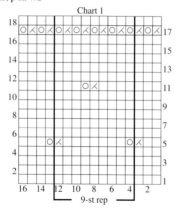

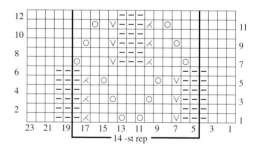

### Stitch Key

☐ K on RS, p on WS

Ⓞ Yo

☒ K2tog

### Stitch Key

☐ K on RS, p on WS

⊟ P on RS, k on WS

Ⓞ Yo

☒ K2tog

☑ K2tog tbl

## HOOD

With larger needles, cast on 120 (124, 128, 132) sts.

### Beg chart

**Row 1 (RS)** Beg with st 1 (21, 19, 17) work to st 22, work sts 1 to 22 for 5 (6, 6, 6) times, end with st 10 (12, 14, 16). Cont in pat as established until piece measures 2 (2¼, 2½, 2¾)"/5 (5.5, 6.5, 7)cm from beg.

### Top shaping

Dec 1 st each side every other row 31 times, bind off 2 sts at beg of next 20 (22, 24, 26) rows. Work even until piece measures 9 (9½, 10, 10½)"/23 (24, 25.5, 26.5)cm from beg. Bind off rem 18 sts.

## FINISHING

Block pieces to measurements. Sew shoulder seams. Sew hood around neck as foll: sew from A to B from front neck edge to shoulder; from B to C from shoulder to center back neck. Sew back hood seam from C to D.

### Ribbed edge

With RS facing and circular needle, pick up and k 78 (86, 94, 104) sts along right front edge, 136 (140, 144, 148) sts along outside edge of hood and 78 (86, 94, 104) sts along left front edge— 292 (312, 332, 356) sts. Work in k2, p2 rib for 1 row. Place markers on left front band for 5 buttonholes, the first one at ½"/1.5cm from lower edge, the last one just below neck shaping, and three other spaced evenly between. Work buttonhole on next row at markers as foll: bind off 1 st. On foll row, cast on 1 st. Rib 1 row even. Bind off in rib.

Set in sleeves. Sew side and sleeve seams. Make a tassel and sew to point of hood.

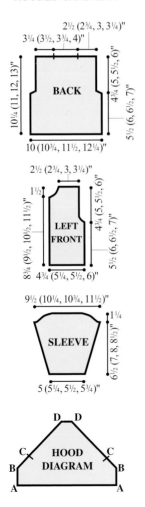

HOODED CARDIGAN

BACK

2½ (2¾, 3, 3¼)"
3¼ (3½, 3¾, 4)"
10¼ (11, 12, 13)"
4¾ (5, 5½, 6)"
5½ (6, 6½, 7)"
10 (10¾, 11½, 12¼)"

LEFT FRONT

2½ (2¾, 3, 3¼)"
1½
8¾ (9½, 10½, 11½)"
4¾ (5, 5½, 6)"
4¾ (5¼, 5½, 6)"
5½ (6, 6½, 7)"

SLEEVE

9½ (10¼, 10¾, 11½)"
1¼
6½ (7, 8, 8½)"
5 (5¼, 5½, 5¾)"

HOOD DIAGRAM
D  D
C  C
B  B
A  A

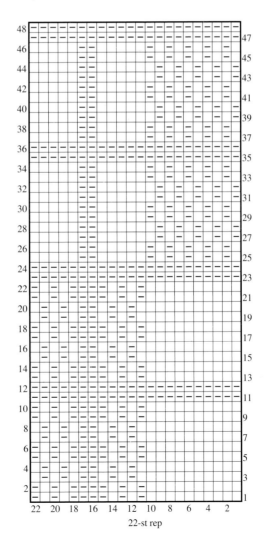

22-st rep

**Stitch Key**

☐ K on RS, p on WS

⊟ P on RS, k on WS

# Go Fish

Get into the swim of things! Sporting intarsia fish motifs, easy-access button closures on the shoulders and self-finished rolled edges, these sassy sweaters stitch up quick in stockinette. "Go Fish" first appeared in the Fall '01 issue of *Family Circle Easy Knitting* magazine.

## MATERIALS

■ *Sesia Baby* by Sesia/Colorado Yarns, 1³/₄oz/50g skeins, each approx 192yd/178m (cotton)

*White version*

   2 (3, 4) skeins in #51 white (MC)

   1 (1, 1) skein each in #487 green (A), #86 dk blue (B) and #550 med blue (C)

*Green version*

   2 (3, 4) skeins in #487 green (MC)

   1 (1, 1) skein each in #51 white (A), #550 med blue (B) and #86 dk blue (C)

■ One pair size 4 (3.5mm) needles OR SIZE TO OBTAIN GAUGE

■ Size D/3 (3mm) crochet hook

■ Two ⁵/₈"/15mm buttons

## SIZES

Sized for Child's 3-6 months (9-12 months, 18-24 months). Shown in size 9-12 months.

## FINISHED MEASUREMENTS

■ Chest 22 (25, 28)"/56 (63.5, 71)cm

■ Length 11 (12¹/₂, 14)"/28 (31.5, 35.5)cm

■ Upper arm 10 (11¹/₂, 13)"/25.5 (29, 33)cm

## GAUGE

25 sts and 32 rows to 4"/10cm over St st using size 4 (3.5mm) needles.
TAKE TIME TO CHECK YOUR GAUGE.

## BACK

With smaller needles and MC, cast on 68 (78, 88) sts. Work in St st for 6 (6³/₄, 7¹/₂)"/15.5 (17, 19)cm, end with a WS row.

**Armhole shaping**

**Next (dec) row (RS)** K1, SKP, k to last 3 sts, k2tog, k1. Rep dec row every 6th (8th, 10th) rows 4 times more—58 (68, 78) sts. Work even until piece measures 11 (12¹/₂, 14)"/28 (31.5, 35.5)cm from beg, end with a WS row. **Next row (RS)** Bind off 41 (47, 53) sts, work on rem 17 (21, 25) sts in St st for ³/₄"/2cm for button flap. Bind off.

## FRONT

Work same as back until piece measures 3¹/₂ (4¹/₂, 5)"/9 (11, 13)cm from beg, end with a WS row.

**Beg chart**

**Next row (RS)** Work 21 (26, 31) sts, work chart row 1 over next 25 sts, work to end. Cont as established through chart row 27, (work armhole shaping on RS rows as for back) then cont with MC only until piece measures 9¹/₂ (11, 12¹/₂)"/24 (28, 31.5)cm from beg, end with a WS row.

**Neck shaping**

**Next row (RS)** Bind off center 10 (12, 14) sts, work to end. Working both sides at once, bind off from each neck edge 3 sts once, 2 sts once, 1 st twice. Work even on rem 17 (21, 25) sts each side until piece measures 11 (12¹/₂, 14)"/28 (31.5, 35.5)cm from beg. Bind off rem sts each side.

## SLEEVES

With smaller needles and MC, cast on 46 (50, 54) sts. Work in St st, inc 1 st each side every 4th row 8 (11, 14) times—62 (72, 82) sts. Work even until piece measures 5 (6¹/₂, 8)"/12.5 (16.5, 20.5)cm from beg.

**Cap shaping**

Bind off 6 sts at beg of next 6 rows. Bind off rem 26 (36, 46) sts.

## FINISHING

Block pieces to measurements. Sew right shoulder seam.

**Neckband**

With RS facing, smaller needles and MC, beg at left front shoulder, pick up and k 1 st in each st and row around front and back neck edge (including side of button flap). Work in St st for ³/₄"/2cm. Bind off. With RS facing, crochet hook and MC, work a row of MC along top of back button flap and side of neckband, working two ch-3 button loops evenly spaced (see photo). Sew buttons to front opposite loops. Set in sleeves. Sew side and sleeve seams.

*(See schematics and chart on page 120)*

# Patchwork Pleaser

A bear necessity—this delightful teddy bear dress and hat set designed by Nicky Epstein uses simple colorwork, textural stitches and embroidery to duplicate the look of a much-loved quilt. "Patchwork Pleaser" first appeared in the Winter '96/'97 issue of *Family Circle Knitting* magazine.

## MATERIALS

- *Handicrafter Cotton* by Bernat® 1¾oz/50g skein, each approx 80yd/73m

  4 skeins each #85 beige (A), #02 cream (B), #83 periwinkle (C), #89 yellow (D), #91 moss green (E), #14 coral (F), #13 bright pink (G), #97 lavender (H), #87 jade (I)
- One pair each size 4 and 5 (3.5 and 3.75 mm) needles OR SIZE TO OBTAIN GAUGE
- Four ⅝"/15mm buttons
- Stitch holders
- Stitch markers
- Yarn needle

## SIZES

Sized for 2 (4, 6). Shown in size 2.

## FINISHED MEASUREMENTS

- Chest 23 (24, 26)"/58.5 (61, 66)cm
- Length 19½ (20, 20½)"/49.5 (51, 52)cm
- Width at upperarm 10 ½ (11, 11½)"/27 (28, 29)cm

## GAUGE

22 sts and 30 rows to 4"/10 cm in St st using larger needles.
TAKE TIME TO CHECK YOUR GAUGE.

## STITCHES

**Seed st** (any number of sts)
**Row 1** * K1, p1; rep from *. **Row 2** K the purl sts and p the knit sts. Rep row 2 for seed st pat.

**Knot st** (odd number of sts)
**Rows 1 and 3 (RS)** With MC, knit. **Rows 2 and 4** With MC purl. **Row 5** With CC k1, (k1, yo, k1) all in next st, * sl 1, (k1, yo, k1) all in next st; rep from * to last st, k1. **Row 6** With CC k1, k3tog through back lp (tbl), * sl 1, k3tog tbl; rep from * to last st, k1. Rep rows 1-6 for knot st pat.

**Scallop**
Cast on 4 sts.
**Row 1** Knit. **Row 2** Cast on 1 st at beg of row, k to end. Rep row 2 until there are 10 sts. K 2 rows. Place sts on holder.

## FRONT

With smaller needles and A, cast on 105 sts. K 12 rows. Change to larger needles.

## FIRST BLOCK BAND

**Next row (RS)** With F as (MC) and B as (CC), work Chart #1 over 21 sts; with E work in Seed st pat over 21 sts; with H work in St st over 21 sts; with D as (MC), work row 1 of Knot st pat over 21 sts; with G as (MC) and C as (CC), work Chart #2 over 21 sts. Cont in pat as established until 30 rows have been completed. **Note:** Work 6 rows of Knot st pat 5 times, alternating (CC) by working rows 5 and 6 first with F, then C, then E, then H, and then B.

## SECOND BLOCK BAND

**Next row (RS)** With C, work in St st over 21 sts; with A as (MC), work row 1 of Knot st pat over 21 sts; Work in St st over next 21 sts as foll: 7 sts with G, 7 sts with D and 7 sts with E; With F as (MC) and C as (CC), work Chart #3 over 21 sts; With B as (MC) and H as (CC), work Chart #4 over 21 sts. Cont in pat as established until 30 rows have been completed.
**Note:** Alternate (CC) of Knot st pat by working rows 5 and 6 with D, H, I, F, then B.

## THIRD BLOCK BAND

With G as (MC) and C as (CC), Work Chart #2 over 21 sts; with H as (MC) and D as (CC), work Chart #3 over 21 sts; with C, work in Seed st pat over 21 sts; With B as (MC) and E as (CC), work Chart #1 over 21 sts; with I, work in St st over 21 sts. Cont in pat as established until 30 rows have been completed, AT SAME TIME, dec 1 st each side every 4th (6th, 6th) row 6 (4, 2) times—93 (97, 101) sts.

### Beg Bodice

**Next row (RS)** With A, knit, dec 30 sts evenly across—63 (67, 71) sts. P next row. With A as (MC), work Knot st pat over 21 (23, 25) sts; with E as (MC) and F as (CC), work Chart #3 over 21 sts; with A as (MC); work Knot st pat over 21 (23, 25) sts. Cont in pat as established. **Note:** Alternate (CC) of Knot st pat by working rows 5 and 6 with G, H, E, B, then C, AT SAME TIME, when bodice measures 1½"/4cm, end with a WS row and work as foll:

### Armhole shaping

Bind off 4 (5, 6) sts at beg of next 2 rows, 2 sts at beg of next 2 rows—51 (53, 55) sts. Work even until armhole measures 3 (3½, 4)"/7.5 (9, 10)cm, AT SAME TIME when 30 rows of Chart #3 have been completed, cont Knot st pat across all sts on needle, using F, D and I for CC stripes.

*(Continued on page 120)*

Visions of sugarplums will dance in her head when she puts on this adorable confection. Sugar cookie motifs are duplicate stitched over stockinette; eyelet lace adds something special to the sleeves, neck and hem. "Sweet Treat" first appeared in the Spring/Summer '99 issue of *Family Circle Easy Knitting* magazine.

## MATERIALS

- *Cablé 5* by Mondial/Skacel Collections, 1¾oz/50g balls, each approx 216yd/200m (cotton)
  2 (2, 3) balls in #100 white (A)
  2 (2, 2) balls in #635 aqua (B)
- *Anchor Embroidery Floss* by Coats & Clark, each skein approx 8yd/7m (cotton)
- 1 skein each in #365 carmel; #363 lt carmel; #295 yellow; #398 grey; #1 white; #9046 red; #11 dk pink; #361 champagne; #292 lt yellow; #54 dk rose; #52 rose; #50 lt. rose; #901 dk beige; #301 lt yellow; #891 beige; #379 brown beige; #376 lt brown beige; #323 orange; #324 dk orange; #6 pale pink; #386 ivory; #375 dk pale brown; #373 pale brown; #9 pink for embroidery
- One pair size 1 and 2 (2.25 and 2.5mm) needles OR SIZE TO OBTAIN GAUGE
- Stitch holder
- Three ¼"/6mm buttons

## SIZES

Sized for Baby's 12 (18, 24) months. Shown in size 12 month.

## FINISHED MEASUREMENTS

- Chest 23½ (25, 27)"/59.5 (63.5, 68.5)cm
- Length 10½ (12, 13)"/26.5 (30.5, 33)cm
- Upper arm 9½ (10½, 11)"/24 (26.5, 28)cm

## GAUGE

30 sts and 42 rows to 4"/10cm over St st using larger needles and 2 strands of yarn.
TAKE TIME TO CHECK YOUR GAUGE.

### Notes

**1** Work with 2 strands of yarn held tog throughout.
**2** Cookie motifs are embroidered in duplicate st after pieces are knit.

### Lace Pattern 1

(multiple of 9 plus 2)
**Row 1 (RS)** K1, p to last st, k1. **Row 2** Knit.
**Row 3** K1, SKP, k2, yo, *k1, yo, k2, k2tog, SKP, k2, yo; rep from *, end k1, yo, k2, k2tog, k1. **Row 4** Rep row 1. **Row 5** Rep row 3. **Row 6** Rep row 1. **Row 7** Rep row 3. **Row 8** Rep row 1. Rep rows 1-8 for lace pat 1.

### Lace pattern 2

(multiple of 6 plus 3)

**Row 1 (RS)** Knit. **Row 2 and all WS rows** Purl. **Row 3** Knit. **Row 5** *K4, yo, SKP; rep from * to last 3 sts, k3. **Row 7** K2, k2tog, yo, k1, yo, SKP, *k1, k2tog, yo, k1, yo, SKP; rep from * to last 2 sts, k2. **Rows 9 and 11** Knit. **Row 13** K1, yo, SKP, *k4, yo, SKP; rep from * to end. **Row 15** K2, yo, SKP, k1, k2tog, yo, *k1, yo, SKP, k1, k2tog, yo; rep from *, to last 2 sts, k2. **Row 16** Purl.
Rep rows 1-16 for lace pat 2.

### RIB/LACE PATTERN

(multiple of 6 sts plus 1)
**Rows 1 and 3 (WS)** P1, *k1, p3, k1, p1; rep from * to end.
**Row 2** *K1, p1, k2tog, yo, k1, p1; rep from *, end k1.
**Row 4** *K1, p1, k3, p1; rep from *, end k1.
Rep rows 1-4 for rib/lace pat.

### BACK

With smaller needles and 2 strands A, cast on 83 (92, 101) sts. Work lace pat 1 (foll written instructions or chart) for 10 rows, inc 5 (inc 2, dec 1) st on last row—88 (94, 100) sts. Change to larger needles and work in St st until piece measures 10½ (12, 13)"/26.5 (30.5, 33)cm from beg, end with a WS row.
**Next row (RS)** Bind off 28 (30, 32) sts for right

shoulder, place center 32 (34, 36) sts on a holder for neck, work on rem 28 (30, 32) sts for left shoulder for 8 rows more for button flap. Bind off.

### FRONT

Work as for back until piece measures 9 (10½, 11½)"/22.5 (26.5, 29)cm from beg, end with a RS row.

**Neck shaping**

**Next row (RS)** Work 38 (40, 42) sts, join 2nd ball of yarn and bind off center 12 (14, 16) sts for neck, work to end. Working both sides at once, bind off from each neck edge 3 sts once, 2 sts twice, 1 st 3 times, AT SAME TIME, when piece measures 9¾ (11¼, 12¼)"/24.5 (28.5, 31)cm from beg, work two buttonholes on left shoulder as foll: At beg of a RS row, k8, k to last 11 sts, bind off 2 sts, work to end. On next row, cast on 2 sts over bound-off sts. Work even until piece measures same length as back. Bind off rem 28 (30, 32) sts each side for shoulders.

### SLEEVES

With smaller needles and 2 strands A, cast on 51 sts. Beg with a p row, work in St st for 8 rows. K next row on WS for turning ridge. Work in St st for 8 rows. Change to larger needles and 2 strands B. Work in lace pat 2, (foll written
*(Continued on page 122)*

# Special Delivery

for intermediate knitters

Snuggly soft sweaters are sure to delight and inspire. Tiny hearts wrap the waist of the striped side-button vest sweetened with lacy picot edges. The ultra-soft pullover sports a simple Fair Isle pattern, pretty picot edging and a simple three-button closure. "Special Delivery" first appeared in the Fall '99 issue of *Family Circle Easy Knitting* magazine.

## MATERIALS

*Pullover*

- Peter Pan DK by Wendy/Berroco, Inc., 1³/₄oz/50g balls, each approx 184yd/170m (nylon/acrylic) 2 balls each in #301 ecru (MC) and #998 blue (CC)
- One pair each sizes 2 and 4 (2.5 and 3.5mm) needles OR SIZE TO OBTAIN GAUGE
- Three ¹/₂"/13mm buttons

*Vest*

  2 balls in #301 ecru (MC)
  1 (2, 2) balls in #998 blue (CC)
- One pair each sizes 2 and 4 (2.5 and 3.5mm) needles OR SIZE TO OBTAIN GAUGE
- Size C/2 (2.5mm) crochet hook
- Three ¹/₂"/13mm buttons

## SIZES

Sized for 3 (6, 9) months. Shown in size 6 months.

## PULLOVER

### FINISHED MEASUREMENTS

- Chest 21¹/₂ (23, 25)"/54.5 (58.5, 63.5)cm
- Length 9¹/₂ (10¹/₂, 11³/₄)"/24 (27, 30)cm
- Upper arm 10 (11, 11¹/₂)"/25 (28, 29)cm

### GAUGE

25 sts and 34 rows to 4"/10cm over St st and chart pat using larger needles.
TAKE TIME TO CHECK YOUR GAUGE.

### Note

All measurements on schematics reflect the measurement "above" the eyelet row.

### BACK

With smaller needles and MC, cast on 67 (73, 79) sts. P 1 row, k 1 row, p 1 row. **Eyelet Row (RS)** *K2tog, yo; rep from *, end k1. Work 3 rows in St st. Change to larger needles. Work 4 rows St st, 2 rows garter st, 2 rows St st.

### Beg polka dot chart

**Row 1 (RS)** Work 6-st rep (sts 1-6) 11 (12, 13) times, end with st 7. Cont in pat as established

until piece measures 6¹/₂ (7¹/₂, 8³/₄)"/16 (19, 22)cm above eyelet row.

### Placket shaping

**Next row (RS)** Work 33 (36, 39) sts, join 2nd ball of yarn and bind off center st, work to end. Work both sides at once with separate balls of yarn until piece measures 9¹/₂ (10¹/₂, 11³/₄)"/24 (27, 30)cm above eyelet row. Bind off sts each side.

### FRONT

Work as for back until piece measures 8¹/₂ (9¹/₂, 10³/₄)"/21 (24, 27)cm above eyelet row, end with a WS row.

### Neck shaping

**Next row (RS)** Work 29 (31, 33) sts, join 2nd ball of yarn and bind off center 9 (11, 11) sts, work to end. Working both sides at once with separate balls, bind off from each neck edge 3 sts once, 2 sts once, dec 1 st every other row twice. When same length as back, bind off rem 22 (24, 27) sts each side for shoulders.

### SLEEVES

With MC, cast on 39 (41, 43) sts. Work first 15 rows as for back.

### Beg polka dot chart

**Row 1 (RS)** Work beg with st 3 (2, 1) work to st

6, work 6-st rep 5 (6, 6) times, end with st 5 (6, 7). Cont in pat as established, inc 1 st each side (working inc sts into chart pat) every other row 6 (8, 4) times, every 4th row 6 (6, 11) times—63 (69, 73) sts. Work even until piece measures 6¹/₂ (7, 8¹/₄)"/16 (18, 21)cm above eyelet row. Bind off all sts.

### FINISHING

Block pieces to measurements. Sew shoulder seams.

### Neckband

With RS facing and MC, pick up and k 59 (63, 63) sts evenly around neck edge. K 1 row on WS. Work in St st for 3 rows. Work eyelet row as for back. Work in St st for 3 rows. Bind off. Fold band in half to WS at eyelet row and sew in place.

### Placket band

With RS facing, crochet hook and MC, work 1 row sc and 1 row backwards sc (from left to right) along each placket edge, making 3 ch-3 loops evenly along right placket edge.

Place markers 5 (5¹/₂, 5³/₄)"/12.5 (14, 14.5)cm down from shoulder seams on front and back. Sew top of sleeves between markers. Sew side

*(Continued on page 123)*

A cool cotton romper and matching rolled-brim hat in perky pastel shades inspire lots of fun in the sun. They knit up quick and easy in stockinette stripes; garter stitch trim decorates the edges. Designed by Kirsten Cowan, "Beach Babe" first appeared in the Spring/Summer '01 issue of *Family Circle Easy Knitting* magazine.

## MATERIALS

- *Windsurf* by Sesia/Colorado Yarns, 1¾oz/50g balls, each approx 119yd/108m (cotton)
  2 (3, 4) balls each in #89 lilac (MC), #99 yellow (A) and #148 green (B)
- One pair size 6 (4mm) needles OR SIZE TO OBTAIN GAUGE
- Four ⅝"/15mm buttons

## SIZES

Sized for 6 (12, 18) months. Shown in size 6 months.

## FINISHED MEASUREMENTS

- Chest 20 (22, 24)"/51 (56, 61)cm
- Length 14 (15, 16½)"/35.5 (38, 42)cm
- Hat circumference 16 (17, 18)"/40.5 (43, 45.5)cm

## GAUGE

22 sts and 30 rows to 4"/10cm over St st using size 6 (4mm) needles.
TAKE TIME TO CHECK YOUR GAUGE.

**Note**

When changing colors, twist yarns tog on WS to prevent holes.

## RIGHT FRONT

With MC, cast on 28 (31, 32) sts. Work 5 rows in garter st. **Next row (RS)** With MC, k9 (10, 10), with A, k19 (21, 22). Cont in St st as established for 3 more rows. **Next row (RS)** With MC, k1, inc 1 st, k to last 2 sts in MC, inc 1 st, k1; with A, k1, inc 1 st, k to last 2 sts, inc 1 st, k1. Work 3 rows even. Rep last 4 rows 3 (4, 5) times more—44 (51, 56) sts. **Next row (RS)** Work even to last 2 sts, inc 1 st (for side seam), k1. Work 3 rows even. Rep last 4 rows 2 (1, 2) times more and AT SAME TIME, when piece measures 3½ (4,

4½)"/9 (10, 11.5)cm, shape crotch by binding off 1 st at beg of every RS row 4 (5, 5) times—43 (48, 54) sts. Work even until piece measures 7 (8, 9)"/18 (20.5, 23)cm from beg. **Next row (RS)** K to last 2 sts in MC, k2tog; with A, SKP, k to end. Work 3 rows even. Rep last 4 rows 7 (8, 9) times more and AT SAME TIME, work armhole shaping when piece measures 11 (11½, 12½)"/28 (29, 32)cm.

### Armhole shaping

**Next row (WS)** Bind off 4 sts, work to end. Cont to shape armhole binding off 3 sts once, 2 sts once, dec 1 st every other row 2 (3, 5) times—16 (18, 20) sts. Work even if necessary, until armhole measures 1½ (2, 2½)"/3 (5, 6.5)cm.

### Neck shaping

**Next row (RS)** Bind off 4 (6, 7) sts, work to end. Cont to bind off from neck edge, 3 sts once, 2 sts once then dec 1 st every other row 1 (1, 2) times—6 sts. Work even until armhole measures 3 (3½, 4)"/7.5 (9, 10)cm.

### Shoulder shaping

From armhole edge, bind off 2 sts every other row 3 times.

## LEFT FRONT

Work to correspond to right front reversing shaping and working first section with B and 2nd section with MC (see photo).

## LEFT BACK

With MC, cast on 31 (33, 34) sts. Work 5 rows in garter st. **Next row (RS)** With MC, k12, with A, k19 (21, 22). Cont in St st as established for 3 more rows. **Next row (RS)** With MC, k1, inc 1 st, k to last 2 sts in MC, inc 1 st, k1; with A, k1, inc 1 st, k to last 2 sts, inc 1 st, k1. Work 3 rows even. Rep last 4 rows 4 (5, 6) times more—51 (57, 62) sts. **Next row (RS)** Work even to last 2 sts, inc 1 st (for side seam), k1. Work 3 rows even. Rep last 4 rows 1 (0, 1) time, AT SAME TIME, when piece measures 3½ (4, 4½)"/9 (10, 11.5)cm, shape crotch by binding off 3 sts at beg of next RS row then bind off 1 st at beg of every RS row 5 times more—45 (50, 56) sts. Work even until piece measures 6 (7, 8)"/15 (18, 20.5)cm from beg. **Next row (RS)** Bind off 2 sts (for back band)—43 (48, 54) sts. Work even until piece measures 7 (8, 9)"/18 (20.5, 23)cm from beg. **Next row (RS)** K to last 2 sts in MC, k2tog; with A, SKP, k to end. Work 3 rows even. Rep last 4 rows 7 (8, 9) times more, AT SAME TIME, when piece measures 11 (11½, 12½)"/28 (29, 32)cm, work as foll:

### Armhole shaping

**Next row (WS)** Bind off 4 sts, work to end. Cont to shape armhole binding off 3 sts once, 2 sts once, dec 1 st every other row 3 (4, 6) times—

*(Continued on page 124)*

Just like Mom's: Cheerful bands of color jazz up Baby's relaxed dropped-shoulder pullover. Designed by Barbara Venishnick, the sweater knits up in a flash with two strands of yarn held together. "Lucky Stripes" first appeared in the Spring/Summer '02 issue of *Family Circle Easy Knitting* magazine.

## MATERIALS

- *Saucy* by Reynolds/JCA, 3½oz/100g balls, each approx 185yd/170m (cotton)
  2 (3, 3) balls in #800 white (MC)
  1 ball each in #361 red (A), #365 pink (B), #372 hot pink (C) and #612 dk pink (D)
- One pair size 10½ (7mm) needles OR SIZE TO OBTAIN GAUGE
- Size 10½ (7mm) circular needle, 16"/40cm long
- Stitch holders

## SIZES

Sized for Child's 2 (4, 6). Shown in size 2.

## FINISHED MEASUREMENTS

- Chest 27 (29, 32)"/68.5 (74, 81)cm
- Length 12½ (13½, 14½)"/32 (34, 37)cm
- Upper arm 11 (12, 13)"/28 (30.5, 33)cm

## GAUGE

12 sts and 19 rows to 4"/10cm over St st using 2 strands of yarn and size 10½ (7mm) needles. TAKE TIME TO CHECK YOUR GAUGE.

### Note

Work with 2 strands of yarn held tog throughout. To make this easier, work with 1 strand from center and 1 strand from outside of a single ball.

## BACK

With 2 strands of MC, cast on 40 (44, 48) sts, purl 1 row.

### Beg stripe pat

**Row 1 (RS)** K20 (22, 24) with A, k20 (22, 24) with MC. **Row 2** Purl, matching colors. **Row 3** K20 (22, 24) with MC, k20 (22, 24) with B. **Row 4** Purl, matching colors. Rep these 4 rows for stripe pat until piece measures 11 (12, 13)"/28

(30.5, 33)cm from beg, end with a RS row.

### Neck and shoulder shaping

**Next row (WS)** P13 (14, 15), place center 14 (16, 18) sts on a holder for neck, join double strand of yarn and p to end. Working both sides at once, dec 1 st at each neck edge every other row twice. Work even until piece measures 12½ (13½, 14½)"/32 (34, 37)cm from beg. Bind off rem 11 (12, 13) sts each side for shoulders.

## FRONT

Work as for back. Block pieces to measurements. Sew shoulder seams.

## SLEEVES

### Note

Make 1 sleeve using MC and C, 1 sleeve using MC and D.

Place markers at 5½ (6, 6½)"/14 (15, 16.5)cm down from shoulders on front and back. With 2 strands of MC, pick up and k 35 (37, 39) sts between markers (working approx 3 sts for every 4 rows). P 1 row with MC. Then cont in stripe pat of 2 rows C (or D) and 2 rows MC for a total of 7 rows from pick-up row. Dec 1 st each side of next row then every 8th row twice

more—29 (31, 33) sts. Work even on 29 (31, 33) sts until there are 15 (15, 17) stripes completed in stripe pat. Bind off loosely.

## FINISHING

Block to measurements. Sew side and sleeve seams.

### Neckband

With circular needle and 2 strands of MC, pick up and k 34 (38, 42) sts evenly around neck edge. Join and working in rnds, k4 rnds. Bind off loosely.

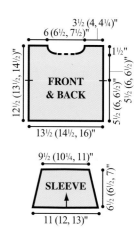

What could be more comfortable than this classic footed romper? Fetching pastel stripes enhance Abigail Lile's darling design featuring a back closure, soft stripes and fine ribbing at the yoke, collar and cuffs. "Romper Room" first appeared in the Spring/Summer '01 issue of *Family Circle Easy Knitting* magazine.

## MATERIALS

- *Windsurf* by Sesia/Colorado Yarns, 1¾oz/50g balls, each approx 119yd/108m (cotton)
  4 balls in #148 green (MC)
  3 balls in #203 blue (CC)
- One pair each sizes 5 and 6 (3.75 and 4mm) needles OR SIZE TO OBTAIN GAUGE
- Nine ½"/13mm buttons

## SIZES

Sized for 6-12 months.

## FINISHED MEASUREMENTS

- Chest 30½"/77.5cm
- Length 19½"/49.5cm
- Upper arm 9¼"/23.5cm

## GAUGE

22 sts and 30 rows to 4"/10cm over St st using larger needles.
TAKE TIME TO CHECK YOUR GAUGE.

## FRONT

### First leg

Beg at foot with smaller needles and MC, cast on 2 sts.
**Row 1 (RS)** Inc 1 st in each st—4 sts. **Row 2** [Inc 1 st in first st, p1] twice. **Row 3** Inc 1 st in first st, k3, inc 1 st in next st, k1. **Row 4** Inc 1 st in first st, p5, inc 1 st in next st, p1. **Rows 5-8** Cont to inc 1 st at beg and end of each row as on previous rows—18 sts. Work even until foot measures 4"/10cm from beg, end with a RS row.
**Next row (WS)** Bind off 3 sts (inside of leg), p to end. Change to larger needles and CC. **Inc row (RS)** K1, k into front, back and front of each st across to last st, k1—41 sts. Beg with a p row, work 7 rows with CC in St st. Working in St st, work 8 rows MC, 8 rows CC and 8 rows MC. K1 row with CC. Sl sts to a holder.

### Second leg

Work as for first leg on 18 sts for 4"/10cm. **Next row (WS)** Work to last 3 sts, with separate length of yarn, bind off last 3 sts (inside of leg). Then cont as first leg on 41 sts until there are 4 stripes. K1 row with CC.

### Join legs

**Next row (WS)** P 41 sts of second leg, cast on 2 sts for crotch, working sts of first leg from holder, p to end—84 sts. Work 6 more rows in St st with CC. *Work 8 rows MC, 8 rows CC; rep from * once. Work 8 rows MC.

### YOKE

**Row 1 (RS)** With CC, knit. Row 2 With CC, *k1, p1; rep from * to end. Rep last row 6 times more. With MC, rep last 8 rows once.

### Armhole shaping

Cont in 16 rows of stripe and rib pat, bind off 2 sts at beg of next 2 rows, dec 1 st each side every row 4 times—72 sts. Work even until armhole measures 2¼"/6cm, end with last row of MC stripe.

### Neck shaping

**Next row** Work 33 sts, join another ball of yarn and bind off 6 sts, work to end. Working both sides at once, bind off 2 sts from each neck edge twice, dec 1 st every other row 5 times—24 sts rem each side. Work even until armhole measures 4½"/11.5cm. Bind off sts each side for shoulders.

### BACK

Work as for front to yoke.

### Back opening

**Next row (RS)** K39, with separate ball of yarn bind off 6 sts, k to end. Cont to work each side separately until same length as front to armhole. Work armhole shaping on each side as on front—33 sts each side. Work even until armhole measures 3½"/9cm.

### Neck shaping

Bind off 5 sts from each neck edge once, 4 sts once. When same length as front, bind off 24 sts each side for shoulders.

### SLEEVES

With smaller needles and MC, cast on 35 sts. Work in k1, p1 rib for 3"/9cm. Change to larger needles and cont in St st and stripe pat of 8 rows CC, 8 rows MC, AT SAME TIME, inc 1 st each side every 4th row 8 times—51 sts. Work even until piece measures 5"/12.5cm above ribbed cuff.

### Cap shaping

Dec 1 st each side of next row and every other row twice more—45 sts. Bind off.

*(Continued on page 124)*

A bright-on-bright sweater, trimmed with picot hem edgings and shoulder button plackets, makes an eye-catching treat for the one who stole your heart. "Heart Warmer" first appeared in the Fall '01 issue of *Family Circle Easy Knitting* magazine.

## MATERIALS

■ *501* by Filatura Di Crosa/Tahki•Stacy Charles, Inc., 1³⁄₄oz/50g skeins, each approx 136yd/125m (wool)

    4 (5, 6) skeins #2150 orange (MC)

    1 (1, 1) skein each of the two contrasting colors: #148 red (A) and #101 white (B)

■ One pair each sizes 4 and 5 (3.5 and 3.75mm) needles OR SIZE TO OBTAIN GAUGE

■ Three ¹⁄₂"/13mm buttons

## SIZES

Sized for Child's 3-6 months (9-12 months, 18-24 months). Shown in size 9-12 months.

## FINISHED MEASUREMENTS

■ Chest 23 (27, 31)"/58.5 (68.5, 78.5)cm

■ Length 12 (13¹⁄₂, 15)"/30 (34, 38)cm

■ Upper arm 10 (11¹⁄₂, 13¹⁄₂)"/25.5 (29, 34.5)cm

## GAUGE

22 sts and 30 rows to 4"/10cm over St st using larger needles.

TAKE TIME TO CHECK YOUR GAUGE.

## BACK

With smaller needles and MC, cast on 64 (74, 84) sts. Work in St st for ³⁄₄"/2cm, end with a WS row.

**Next (eyelet) row (RS)** K1, *yo, k2tog; rep from to last st, k1. Change to larger needles and work in St st until piece measures 12 (13¹⁄₂, 15)"/30.5 (34, 38)cm above eyelet row, end with a WS row.

**Next row (RS)** Bind off 43 (49, 55) sts, work on rem 21 (25, 29) sts in St st for 1"/2.5cm for button flap. Bind off.

## FRONT

Work same as back until piece measures 2³⁄₄ (3¹⁄₂, 4¹⁄₂)"/7 (9, 11.5)cm above eyelet row, end with a WS row.

**Beg chart**

**Next row (RS)** Work 17 (22, 27) sts, work chart row 1 over next 30 sts, work to end. Cont as established through chart row 36, then cont with MC only until piece measures 10¹⁄₂ (12, 13¹⁄₂)"/26.5 (30.5, 34)cm above eyelet row, end with a WS row.

**Neck shaping**

**Next row (RS)** Work 28 (32, 36) sts, join 2nd ball of yarn and bind off center 8 (10, 12) sts, work to end. Working both sides at once, bind off from each neck edge 3 sts once, 2 sts once, 1 st twice. Work even on rem 21 (25, 29) sts each side until piece measures 12 (13¹⁄₂, 15)"/30.5 (34, 38)cm above eyelet row. Bind off rem sts each side.

## SLEEVES

With smaller needles and MC, cast on 40 (42, 44) sts. Work in St st for ³⁄₄"/2cm, end with a WS row.

**Next (eyelet) row (RS)** K1, *yo, k2tog; rep from to last st, k1. Change to larger needles and work in St st, inc 1 st each side every 4th row 7 (11, 12) times, every 2nd row 0 (0, 3) times—54 (64, 74) sts. Work even until piece measures 5¹⁄₂ (7, 8¹⁄₂)"/14 (17.5, 21.5)cm above eyelet row. Bind off.

## FINISHING

Block pieces to measurements. Sew right shoulder seam.

## Neckband

With RS facing, smaller needles and MC, beg at left front shoulder, pick up and k 1 st in each st and row around front and back neck edge (including side of button flap). Work in St st for ³⁄₄"/2cm, end with a WS row. Work eyelet row same as back. Cont in St st for ³⁄₄"/2cm more. Bind off. Fold neckband in half to WS at eyelet row and sew in place.

With RS facing, crochet hook and MC, work a row of MC along top of back buttonflap and side of neckband, working three ch-3 button loops evenly spaced (see photo). Sew buttons to front opposite loops.

Place markers 5 (5³⁄₄, 6³⁄₄)"/12.5 (14.5, 17)cm down from shoulder seams on front and back. Sew top of sleeves between markers. Sew side and sleeve seams. Fold hems at lower edge of body and sleeves to WS as turning ridge and sew in place.

*(See schematics and chart on page 125)*

She'll be tickled pink dressed in this picture-perfect hat and cardigan set by Agi Revesz. A crocheted lace collar and floral buttons accent the easy-to-make cardigan; add a matching floral-trimmed hat to round off the look. "Early Bloomer" first appeared in the Winter '96/'97 issue off *Family Circle Knitting* magazine.

## MATERIALS

- *Grace* by Patons®, 1³⁄₄oz/50g balls each approx 136yd/125m (cotton)
  5 (5, 6, 6) balls in #60005 white (MC)
  1 ball #60416 pink (CC)
- One pair size 6 (4mm) needles OR SIZE TO OBTAIN GAUGE
- Size 5 (1.75mm) crochet hook
- Stitch holder
- 5³⁄₄"/14.5cm plastic rings

## SIZES

To fit sizes 3-6 (9, 12, 18) months. Shown in size 18 months.

## FINISHED MEASUREMENTS

- Chest at underarm 20 (22, 24, 26)"/51 (56, 61, 66)cm
- Length 11 (12, 13¹⁄₂, 14¹⁄₂)"/28 (30.5, 34, 37)cm
- Sleeve width at upper arm 9 (10, 11, 12)"/23 (25.5, 28, 30.5)cm

## GAUGE

22 sts and 40 rows to 4"/10cm over St st using size 6 (4mm) needles.
TAKE TIME TO CHECK YOUR GAUGE

## STITCH GLOSSARY

**Seed St**
**Row 1** *K1, p1; rep from* to end. **Row 2** K the purl sts and p the knit sts. Rep these two rows for pat.

**Sl-s dec** (left-slanting dec, worked on RS)
With right needle behind left needle, insert right needle through back loops of next 2 sts on left needle. K these 2 sts tog.

**Sl-s dec** (left-slanting dec, worked on WS)
With right needle behind left needle, insert right needle into back loop of second st and then into back loop of first st on left needle

which twists 2 sts, purl these 2 sts tog.

**Sdv dec** (double vertical dec, worked on RS)
Insert right needle into next 2 sts on left needle as if you were knitting them tog and slip them to right needle, k next st on left needle, with left needle, pull both slipped sts over knit st. sdv dec (double vertical dec worked on WS) Insert right needle into next 2 sts on left needle one by one as if you were knitting them, slip them to right needle. (2 twisted sts on right needle), sl 2 slipped sts to left needle, keeping them twisted, insert right needle through back loops of second and first slipped sts and sl them tog off left needle. P next st. With left needle, pass 2 slipped sts over purl st and off right needle.

**Dec 1 sc**
Draw up one loop in next 2 sts then draw yarn through all 3 lps on needle.

**Sr-s dec** (right-slanting dec, worked on RS)
Draw up one loop in next 2 sts then draw yarn through

**Sr-s dec** (right-slanting dec, worked on WS)
Slip next st on the LH needle purlwise, then purl one st. With LH needle, pass the slipped st over the purl st and off the RH needle.

## BACK

With MC, cast on 56 (60, 66, 72) sts. Work in

Seed st for 10¹⁄₄ (11¹⁄₄, 12³⁄₄, 13³⁄₄)"/ 26 (28.5, 32.5, 35) cm from beg. Bind off.

## POCKET LINING

(make 2)
With MC, cast on 16 (16, 17, 17) sts. Work in St st for 2 (2¹⁄₂, 2¹⁄₂, 2¹⁄₂)"/5 (5, 6.5, 6.5) cm, end with a WS row. Place all sts on a holder.

## LEFT FRONT

Wit MC, cast on 28 (30, 33, 36) sts. Work in Seed st for 26 (26, 28, 30) rows. **Next row (RS)** Keeping to pat, work first 6 (7, 8, 9) sts, bind off next 16 (16, 17, 18) sts, work to end. **Next row (WS)** Pat 6 (7, 8, 9) sts, work sts from one lining holder, work to end. Cont in pat until piece measures 8¹⁄₄ (9¹⁄₂, 10³⁄₄, 11³⁄₄)"/21 (24, 27.5, 30) cm from beg, end with a RS row.

**Shape neck**

**Next row (WS)** Bind off first 4 (4, 5, 5) sts, work to end. Cont to shape neck by binding off at neck edge 3 sts once, then 2 sts once. Dec 1 st at neck edge 4 times—15 (17, 19, 22) sts. Work even until piece measures same as back. Bind off all sts.

## RIGHT FRONT

Work as for left front reversing all shaping.

## SLEEVES

With smaller needles and MC, cast on 36 (36,

*(Continued on page 126)*

The Tale of
Peter Rabbit

# Crop Duster

## for intermediate knitters

Get a jumper start on your springtime knitting with this sassy striped suit, showcasing a knit pocket, ribbed hems and buttonshoulder straps. Designed by The Sassy Skein, "Crop Duster" first appeared in the Spring/Summer '02 issue of *Family Circle Easy Knitting* magazine.

### MATERIALS
- *Newport* by Classic Elite Yarns, 1¾oz/50g skeins, each approx 70yd/64m (cotton)
  2 (3, 4) skeins in #2085 orange (A)
  2 (2, 3) skeins in #2083 coral (B)
  2 (3, 3) skeins in #2035 celery (C)
  1 (2, 2) skeins each in #2025 gold (D) and #2907 dk green (E)
- One pair size size 8 (5mm) and one circular needle size 8 (5mm) OR SIZE TO OBTAIN GAUGE
- Stitch holders
- Two ⅝"/15mm decorative buttons for shoulder straps
- Decorative buttons for pocket

### SIZES
Sized for Child's 2 (3, 4). Shown in size 2.

### FINISHED MEASUREMENTS
- Waist 22 (23, 24)"/56 (58.5, 61)cm
- Body width 29 (31, 32)"/73.5 (78.5, 81)cm
- Length (buttoned) 19 (21, 22)"/48 (53, 56)cm

### GAUGE
16 sts and 24 rows to 4"/10cm over St st using size 8 (5mm) needles.
TAKE TIME TO CHECK YOUR GAUGE.

### STRIPE PATTERN
With A, work in St st for 20 (22 23) rows.
**Next row** With D, work in k1, p1 rib.
With B, work in St st for 16 (18, 19) rows.
**Next row** With E, work in k1, p1 rib.
With D, work in St st for 14 (16, 17) rows.
**Next row** With C, work in k1, p1 rib.
With E, work in St st for 11 (14, 15) rows.
**Next row** With A, work in k1, p1 rib.
With C, work in St st for 11 (12, 13) rows.
**Next row** With B, work in k1, p1 rib.
With A, work in St st for 9 (10, 10) rows.
**Next row** With D, work in k1, p1 rib.
With B, work in St st for 8 rows.
**Next row** With E, work in k1, p1 rib.

With D, work in St st for 6 rows.
**Next row** With C, work in k1, p1 rib.
With E, work in St st for 6 rows*. (This is end of front.)
For back only—**Next row** With A, work in k1, p1 rib. With C, work button flap foll instructions.

### PANT LEGS
(make 2)
With C and straight needles, cast on 50 (52, 54) sts. Work in k2, p2 rib for 7 rows. With A, work in stripe pat, inc 1 st each side every other row 4 (5, 5) times—58 (62, 64) sts. Work even until piece measures 4 (4½, 5)"/10 (11.5, 12.5)cm from beg.

### Crotch shaping
With RS facing, join sts from each leg onto circular needle—116 (124, 128) sts. Place marker for center back. Join and cont in stripe pat until piece measures 12 (12½, 13)"/30.5 (32, 33)cm from beg.

### Waist shaping
*For Size 2*—**Next rnd** K2, [k2tog, k2] 28 times, k2—88 sts.
*For Size 3*—**Next rnd** [K2, k2tog] 30 times, [k2tog] twice—92 sts.
*For Size 4*—**Next rnd** [K2, k2tog] 32 times—96 sts.

*For all sizes* Work even until piece measures 13 (13½, 14)"/33 (34.5, 35.5)cm from beg.

### Armhole shaping
From center back marker, place 22 (23, 24) sts on a holder, sl 44 (46, 48) sts for front onto straight needles, place rem 22 (23, 24) sts on same holder as first half.

### FRONT
Bind off 2 (2, 3) sts at beg of next 2 rows. Dec 1 st each side every other row twice—36 (38, 38) sts. Work even until piece measures 16 (17, 17½)"/40.5 (43, 44.5)cm from beg.

### Neck shaping
**Next row (RS)** Work 11 sts, bind off center 14 (16, 16) sts, work to end. Working both sides at once, dec 1 st at each each neck edge every other row twice. Work even through end of stripe pat for front (end at *). Bind off rem 9 sts each side.

### BACK
Sl sts from holder to straight needles and work as for front until same length as front to neck.

### Neck shaping
**Next row (RS)** Work 11 sts, bind off center 14 (16, 16) sts, work to end. Working both sides at once, dec 1 st each each neck edge every other

*(Continued on page 125)*

# The Boy's Club

Your small fry deserves gear that looks good and feels great.

# Cable Classics

## for intermediate knitters

This timeless trio pairs rugged good looks with everyday practicality. Rows of easy-to-execute cables enhance the simple silhouette; a button opening at the shoulder makes for quick changes. "Cable Classics" first appeared in the Fall '01 issue of *Family Circle Easy Knitting* magazine.

### MATERIALS

■ *Primo* by Filatura Di Crosa/Tahki•Stacy Charles, Inc., 1³/₄oz/50g balls, each approx 81yd/74m (wool)

4 (5, 5, 6) balls #272 green; OR #263 purple; OR #237 blue
■ One pair each sizes 7 and 9 (4.5 and 5.5mm) needles OR SIZE TO OBTAIN GAUGE
■ Three ¹/₂"/13mm buttons

### SIZES

Sized for Child's 3-6 months (9-12 months, 18-24 months, 3 years). Shown in size 9-12 months.

### FINISHED MEASUREMENTS

■ Chest 21 (24, 28, 31)"/53.5 (61, 71, 78.5)cm
■ Length 11 (12¹/₂, 14, 15¹/₂)"/28 (31.5, 35.5, 39.5)cm
■ Upper arm 9 (10, 11, 12)"/23 (25.5, 28, 30.5)cm

### GAUGE

16 sts and 24 rows to 4"/10cm over seed st using larger needles.
TAKE TIME TO CHECK YOUR GAUGE.

### SEED STITCH

**Row 1 (RS)** *K1, p1; rep from * to end.
**Row 2** K the purl sts and p the knit sts.
Rep row 2 for seed st.

### Cable pattern

(over 8 sts)
**Rows 1 and 5 (RS)** K1, p2, k2, p2, k1.
**Row 2 and all WS rows** K the knit sts and p the purl sts.
**Row 3** K1, p2, k 2nd st in front of first st, then k first st and drop both sts from LH needle, p2, k1.
**Row 6** Rep row 2.
Rep rows 1-6 for cable pat.

### BACK

With smaller needles, cast on 48 (54, 62, 68) sts.

### Beg pats

**Next row (RS)** Work 5 (8, 11, 13) sts seed st, 8 sts cable pat, [7 (7, 8, 9) sts seed st, 8 sts cable pat] twice, 5 (8, 11, 13) sts seed st. Cont in pats as established for 2 rows more, then change to larger needles and cont in pats until piece measures 11 (12¹/₂, 14, 15¹/₂)"/28 (31.5, 35.5, 39.5)cm from beg, end with a WS row.
**Next row (RS)** Bind off 33 (36, 42, 45) sts, work on rem 15 (18, 20, 23) sts in St st for 1"/2.5cm for button flap. Bind off.

### FRONT

Work same as back until piece measures 9¹/₂ (11, 12¹/₂, 14)"/24 (28, 31.5, 35.5)cm from beg, end with a WS row.

### Neck shaping

**Next row (RS)** Work 20 (23, 25, 28) sts, join 2nd ball of yarn and bind off center 8 (8, 12, 12) sts, work to end. Working both sides at once, bind off from each neck edge 2 sts twice, 1 st once, AT SAME TIME, when piece measures 10¹/₂ (12, 13¹/₂, 15)"/27 (30.5, 34.5, 38.5)cm from beg, work 2 buttonholes on left front (yo, k2tog for each buttonhole) with the first one ¹/₄"/1cm from shoulder edge and the other in center of shoulder. Work even on rem 15 (18, 20, 23) sts each side until piece measures 11 (12¹/₂, 14, 15¹/₂)"/28 (31.5, 35.5, 39.5)cm from beg. Bind off rem sts each side.

### SLEEVES

With smaller needles, cast on 30 (30, 32, 32) sts.

### Beg pats

**Next row (RS)** Work 11 (11, 12, 12) sts seed st, 8 sts cable pat, 11 (11, 12, 12) sts seed st. Cont in pats as established for 2 rows more, then change to larger needles and cont in pats, AT SAME TIME, inc 1 st each side (working inc sts into seed st) every 4th row 4 (3, 1, 2) times, every 6th row 0 (3, 6, 7) times—38 (42, 46, 50) sts. Work even until piece measures 5 (6, 7¹/₂, 9¹/₂)"/12.5 (15.5, 19, 24)cm from beg. Bind off.

### FINISHING

Block pieces to measurements. Sew right shoulder seam.

### Neckband

With RS facing and smaller needles, beg at left front shoulder, pick up and k 1 st in each st and row around front and back neck edge (including side of button flap). Work in k1, p1 rib for ¹/₄"/1cm. Work another buttonhole on left front neck at 2 sts from edge. Cont in rib until band measures ³/₄"/2cm. Bind off in rib. Sew buttons to back shoulder edge opposite buttonholes. Place markers 4¹/₂ (5, 5¹/₂, 6)"/11.5 (12.5, 14, 15.5)cm down from shoulder seams on front and back. Sew top of sleeves between markers. Sew side and sleeve seams.

*(Schematics on page 127)*

# Cream of the Crop

for intermediate knitters

Stitch up a country classic. Worked in garter stitch and accented with striped cuffs and wood buttons, this old-fashioned romper will chase the chill on brisk days. "Cream of the Crop" first appeared in the Fall '99 issue of *Family Circle Easy Knitting* magazine.

## MATERIALS

- *Derby* by Grignasco/JCA, 1¾oz/50g skeins, each approx 162yd/150m (wool/acrylic)
  4 (5, 5) skeins in #800 ecru (MC)
  1 skein in #843 tan (CC)
- One pair size 5 (3.75mm) needles OR SIZE TO OBTAIN GAUGE
- Five ½"/13mm buttons
- Stitch holders

## SIZES

Sized for Newborn (6, 12) months. Shown in size 6 months.

## FINISHED MEASUREMENTS

- Chest (buttoned) 21 (22, 24)"/53.5 (56, 61)cm
- Length (shoulder to cuff) 19 (20¾, 22¾)"/48 (53, 57.5)cm
- Upper arm 9 (9½, 10)"/22 (24, 25)cm

## GAUGE

24 sts and 49 rows to 4"/10cm over garter st using size 5 (3.75mm) needles.
TAKE TIME TO CHECK YOUR GAUGE.

## BACK

### Right leg

With MC, cast on 23 (25, 27) sts and work in garter st as foll: [4 rows MC, 2 rows CC] 3 times. Cont in garter st with MC only, inc 1 st at inside leg (end of RS rows) every 8th row 7 (2, 2) times, every 10th row 0 (5, 6) times—30 (32, 35) sts. Work even until piece measures 8½ (9½, 10¼)"/22 (24, 26)cm from beg. Place sts on a holder.

### Left leg

Work to correspond to right leg, reversing inside leg shaping by working incs at beg of RS rows.

### Leg joining

**Next row (RS)** Work sts from right leg holder, cast on 2 sts, work sts from left leg holder—62 (66, 72) sts. Work even on all sts until piece measures 14½ (16, 17¾)"/37 (41, 45)cm from beg.

### Armhole shaping

Bind off 2 (2, 3) sts at beg of next 2 rows. Work even on rem 58 (62, 66) sts until armhole measures 3¾ (4, 4¼)"/9 (10, 10.5)cm.

### Neck shaping

**Next row (RS)** Work 22 (23, 24) sts, join 2nd skein of yarn and bind off center 14 (16, 18) sts for neck, work to end. Working both sides at once with separate skeins of yarn, bind off from each neck edge 3 sts once. When armhole measures 4½ (4¾, 5)"/11 (12, 13)cm, bind off rem 19 (20, 21) sts each side for shoulders.

## RIGHT FRONT

**Note** Work buttonholes on right front for girl's and left front for boy's. The foll instructions are written for girl's.

With MC, cast on 26 (28, 30) sts and work as for left leg of back. After all inside leg incs have been worked, cont on 33 (35, 38) sts until piece measures 9¼ (10¼, 11)"/24 (26, 28)cm from beg, end with a WS row.

**Next (buttonhole) row (RS)** K2, yo, k2tog, k to end. Work 4 more buttonholes spaced 2 (2¼, 2½)"/5 (5.5, 6)cm apart, AT SAME TIME, when same length as back to armhole, shape armhole at beg of a WS row as for back—31 (33, 35) sts. Work even until armhole measures 3 (3¼, 3½)"/7 (8, 9)cm, end with a WS row.

### Neck shaping

**Next row (RS)** Bind off 4 (5, 6) sts (neck edge), work to end. Cont to bind off from neck edge 2 sts twice, dec 1 st every other row 4 times. When armhole measures 4½ (4¾, 5)"/11 (12, 13)cm, bind off rem 19 (20, 21) sts for shoulder.

## LEFT FRONT

Work to correspond to right front, reversing shaping and omitting buttonholes.

## SLEEVES

With MC, cast on 36 (38, 40) sts and work garter st and stripes as for back. Cont in garter st with MC only, inc 1 st each side every 6th row 6 (6, 5) times, every 4th (8th, 8th) row 3 (3, 5) times—54 (56, 60) sts. Work even until piece measures 6½ (7½, 8¼)"/17 (19, 21)cm from beg. Bind off all sts.

## FINISHING

Block pieces to measurements. Sew shoulder seams.

*(Continued on page 127)*

# Whale of a Time

Even if baby isn't ready for the high seas, he'll love this short set. The pullover features a striped sky, friendly whale and ocean waves. A drawstring waistband means added comfort to matching elastic waist shorts. Designed by Amy Bahrt, this set can be paired with the matching afghan shown on page 86. "Whale of a Time" first appeared in the Spring/Summer '02 issue of *Family Circle Easy Knitting* magazine.

## MATERIALS

- *Super 10* by S.R. Kertzer, Ltd., 4oz/125g skeins, each approx 249yd/230m (cotton)
  2 (3, 3) skeins in #3882 blue (A)
  1 skein each in 3423 red (B) and white (C), #3774 green (D), #3039 charcoal (E) and #3546 yellow (F)
- 1yd/1m of waistband elastic ³⁄₄"/20mm wide
- Stitch holder
- Bobbins

## SIZES

Pullover and shorts sized for 1 (2, 3) years. Shown in size 1 year.

## FINISHED MEASUREMENTS

*Pullover*
- Chest 23 (25, 27)"/58.5 (63.5, 68.5)cm
- Length 12 (13, 14)"/30.5 (33, 35.5)cm
- Upper arm 10 (11, 12)"/25.5 (28, 30.5)cm

*Shorts*
- Hip 23 (24, 25)"/58.5 (61, 63.5)cm
- Length 8³⁄₄ (9³⁄₄, 10³⁄₄)"/22 (24.5, 27)cm

## GAUGE

20 sts and 24 rows to 4"/10cm over St st using larger needles.
TAKE TIME TO CHECK YOUR GAUGE.

## STRIPE PATTERN

*2 rows B, 2 rows C; rep from * (4 rows) for stripe pat.

## PULLOVER

**Note** Use a separate bobbin of yarn for each large block of color. When changing colors, twist yarns on WS to prevent holes in work.

## BACK

With larger needles and A, cast on 59 (63, 67) sts. Work in St st for 6 rows. P next row on RS for turning ridge. Cont in St st until piece measures 5½ (6, 6½)"/14 (15.5, 16.5)cm above turning ridge, end with a WS row.

### Beg chart 4

**Next row (RS)** Work 8-st rep of chart 7 (7, 8) times, work first 3 (7, 3) sts of chart once more. Cont as established through row 6. Cont in stripes of 2 rows C, 2 rows B until piece measures 12 (13, 14)"/30.5 (33, 35.5)cm above turning ridge. Bind off all sts.

### FRONT

With larger needles and A, cast on 59 (63, 67) sts. Work in St st for 6 rows. P next row on RS for turning ridge. Cont in St st for 3 rows. **Next (eyelet) row (RS)** K 25 (27, 29), k2tog, yo, k5, yo, k2tog, k 25 (27, 29). Cont in St st until piece measures 2 (2½, 3)"/5 (6.5, 7.5)cm above turning ridge.

### Beg charts

**Row 1 (RS)** Work 22 (24, 26) sts A, work 15 sts of chart 3, work 22 (24, 26) sts A. Cont as established through row 13, AT THE SAME TIME, after 6 rows of chart 3 have been worked, work as foll: **Next row (RS)** Work 8 (10, 12) sts A, 10 sts chart 2, 4 sts A, cont 15 sts chart 3, 4 sts A, 10 sts chart 1, 8 (10, 12) sts A. Cont as established until all charts rows have been worked. Then cont with A over all sts until piece measures 6½ (7, 7½)"/16.5 (17.5, 19)cm above turning ridge, end with a WS row. Mark center 27 sts.

### Beg charts 4 and 5

**Next row (RS)** Beg with the 8th (6th, 4th) st of chart 4, work to marker, sl marker, work 27 sts of chart 5, sl marker, beg with 3rd st of chart, work to end. Cont as established until 6 rows of chart 4 have been worked, then cont these sts in stripe pat and work until 20 rows of chart 5 have been worked. Then cont all sts in stripe pat until piece measures 9 (10, 11)"/23 (25.5, 28)cm above turning ridge.

### Neck shaping

**Next Row (RS)** Work 24 (25, 27) sts, join 2nd ball of yarn and bind off center 11 (13, 13) sts for neck, work to end. Working both sides at once, bind off 3 sts from each neck edge once, 2 sts once, dec 1 st every other row 3 times. Work even until same length as back. Bind off rem 16 (17, 19) sts each side for shoulders.

### SLEEVES

With smaller needles and C, cast on 36 (36, 38) sts. Work in k1, p1 rib for 7 rows, inc 2 (3, 2) sts on last row—38 (39, 40) sts. Change to larger needles. Work in St st and stripe pat, inc 1 st each side every 4th row 0 (4, 7) times, every 6th row 6 (4, 3) times—50 (55, 60) sts. Work even until piece measures 8½ (9, 10)"/21.5 (23, 25.5)cm from beg, end with a full stripe. Bind off in last stripe color.

### FINISHING

Block pieces to measurements. Sew left shoulder seam.

*(Continued on page 128)*

# Springtime Fun

*for beginner knitters*

Pamper a little one with this cotton threesome. The essential short-sleeved pullover, finished with seed-stitch edges, is complemented with matching socks and a cozy hat ringed in reverse stockinette ridges. "Springtime Fun" first appeared in the Spring/Summer '01 issue of *Family Circle Easy Knitting* magazine.

## MATERIALS

■ *Windsurf* by Sesia/Colorado Yarns, 1³/₄oz/50g balls, each approx 119yd/108m (cotton)

*Pullover*

   2 (3, 3) balls in #148 green (MC)

   1 ball in #203 blue (CC)

■ 1 pair each sizes 4 and 5 (3.5 and 3.75mm) needles OR SIZE TO OBTAIN GAUGE

■ Three ¹/₂"/13mm buttons

■ Stitch holders

*Hat*

■ 1 ball each in #148 green (A) and #203 blue (B)

■ One pair size 5 (3.75mm) needles OR SIZE TO OBTAIN GAUGE

*Socks*

■ 1 ball each in #148 green (A) and #203 blue (B)

■ 1 set (4) size 5 (3.75mm) dpn OR SIZE TO OBTAIN GAUGE

■ Stitch markers

## SIZES

Sized for 6-18 months. Shown in size 6 months.

## FINISHED MEASUREMENTS

■ Hat circumference 16"/40.5cm

## GAUGE

24 sts and 28 rows/rnds to 4"/10cm over St st using size 5 (3.75mm) needles.
TAKE TIME TO CHECK YOUR GAUGE.

## HAT

(one size fits all sizes)

Beg at lower edge with size 5 (3.75mm) needles and A, cast on 96 sts. Work in St st for 12 rows. * With B, k2 rows, p1 row, k1 row. With A, work 4 rows in St st. Rep from * (8 rows) for stripe pat until piece measures approx 3¹/₂"/9cm from beg with edge rolled, ending with 5th B ridge stripe. Cont with A only to end of piece.

### Crown shaping

**Next row (RS)** With A, *k1, SKP, k13, k2tog, k1; rep from * 4 times more, end k1. P1 row. **Next row** *K1, SKP, k11, k2tog, k1; rep from * 4 times more, end k1. P1 row. Cont to dec in this way every other row having 2 sts less between dec's every dec row 5 times more—26 sts. P1 row. **Next row** *K1, SK2P, k1; rep from * 4 times more, end k1—16 sts. P1 row. **Next row** K2tog across. Pull yarn through rem 8 sts and draw up tightly. Cut yarn leaving end for sewing.

## FINISHING

Block lightly. Sew back seam reversing at rolled edge.

## SOCKS

### Cuff

Beg at top edge with A, cast on 30 sts on one needle. Divide sts onto 3 needles with 10 sts on each needle. Join, taking care not to twist sts on needles. Mark end of rnd and sl marker every rnd. Work in rnds of k1, p1 rib for 4 rnds. Then *k2 rnds B, k2 rnds A. Rep from * (4 rnds) for stripe pat in St st until piece measures 2¹/₂ (2³/₄, 3)"/6.5 (7, 7.5)cm from beg.

### Heel

With A, work 8 sts from needle 1, place next 2 sts on needle 2, sl first 3 sts from needle 3 onto needle 2 and last 7 sts onto needle 1—15 sts for heel on needle 1, and 15 sts for instep on needle 2. Work back and forth in rows with A on heel sts as foll: **Row 1 (WS)** Purl. **Row 2 (RS)** *K1, sl 1; rep from * to end. Rep these 2 rows 3 times more.

### Turn heel

**Next row (WS)** P9, p2tog, p1, turn.
**Next row** Sl 1, k4, SKP, k1, turn.
**Next row** Sl 1, p5, p2tog, p1, turn.
**Next row** Sl 1, k6, SKP, k1, turn.
**Next row** Sl 1, p7, p2tog, turn.
**Next row** K8, SKP, k1.

### Instep

With A, pick up and k 5 sts along side of heel, k15 instep sts, pick up and k 5 sts along other side of heel—34 sts total. Divide sts onto 3 needles as foll: 10 sts on needle 1, 15 sts on needle 2, 9 sts on needle 3. **Next rnd** K to last 3 sts on needle 1, k2tog, k1; work even on needle 2; k1, SKP, k to end on needle 3. Resume stripe pat and work 1 rnd even. Rep last 2 rnds once more—30 sts. Work even in stripe pat until foot measures 2¹/₂ (2³/₄, 3¹/₄)"/6.5 (7, 8)cm.

*(Continued on page 127)*

# Double Trouble

## for intermediate knitters

Work up this fabulous Fair Isle design for your boy wonder and his best friend. Playful stick figures dance across the yoke of his rolled-neck pullover; Teddy's version omits the stripes and includes a handsome pompom hat. "Double Trouble" first appeared in the Winter '00/'01 issue of *Family Circle Easy Knitting* magazine.

## MATERIALS

- *Knitaly*® by Colorado Yarns, 3½oz/100g balls, approx 215yd/195m (wool)
  - 2 (2, 3) balls in #1415 blue (A)
  - 2 balls in #2425 ecru (B)
- One pair each sizes 6 and 8 (4 and 5mm) needles OR SIZE TO OBTAIN GAUGE
- Circular needle size 6 (4mm) 16"/40cm long

*Bear Sweater and Hat*
  - 1 ball each in #1369 red (A) and #2428 ecru (B)
- One pair size 8 (5mm) needles OR SIZE TO OBTAIN GAUGE

## SIZES

Sized for Child's 2 (4, 6). Shown in size 4.

## FINISHED MEASUREMENTS

- Chest 26 (29, 32)"/66 (73.5, 81.5)cm
- Length 12¾ (14½, 15½)"/32.5 (37, 39.5)cm
- Upper arm 11 (12, 13)"/28 (31, 33)cm

## GAUGE

18 sts and 22 rows to 4"/10cm over St st and chart pats using larger needles.
TAKE TIME TO CHECK YOUR GAUGE.

## BACK

With smaller needles and A, cast on 59 (65, 73) sts. Work in k1, p1 rib for 1"/2.5cm. Change to larger needles and cont in St st as foll:

### Beg chart

**Row 1 (RS)** Beg with st 7 (4, 12) work to st 17, work 12-st rep (sts 6 to 17) 4 (4, 6) times, end with st 17 (20, 12). Cont in chart as established through row 5, then rep rows 6 to 15 for 2 (3, 3) times, then work rows 16 to 39 once, then rep rows 40 to 51 to end of piece, AT SAME TIME, when piece measures 11¾ (13½, 14½)"/30 (34.5, 37)cm from beg, end with a WS row and work as foll:

### Neck shaping

**Next row (RS)** Work 24 (26, 29) sts, join 2nd ball of yarn and bind off center 11 (13, 15) sts, work to end. Working both sides at once, bind off from each neck edge 3 sts once, 2 sts once. Bind off rem 19 (21, 24) sts each side for shoulders.

## FRONT

Work as for back until piece measures 10¾ (12½, 13½)"/27.5 (32, 34.5)cm from beg, end with a WS row.

### Neck shaping

**Next row (RS)** Work 25 (27, 30) sts, join 2nd ball of yarn and bind off center 9 (11, 13) sts, work to end. Working both sides at once, bind off from each neck edge 3 sts once, 2 sts once, 1 st once. When same length as back, bind off rem 19 (21, 24) sts each side for shoulders.

## SLEEVES

With smaller needles and A, cast on 31 (33, 37) sts. Work in k1, p1 rib for 1"/2.5cm. Change to larger needles and cont in St st as foll:

### Beg chart

**Row 1 (RS)** Beg with st 9 (8, 6) work to st 17, work sts 6 to 17 twice, end with st 15 (16, 18). Cont in chart as established through row 5, then rep rows 6 to 15 for 2 (2, 3) times, then work rows 16 to 39 once, then rep rows 1 to 10 to end of piece, AT SAME TIME, inc 1 st each side every 4th row 2 (6, 1) times, every 6th row 7 (5, 10) times—49 (55, 59) sts. Work even until piece measures 11 (12, 13½)"/28 (30.5, 34.5)cm from beg. Bind off.

## BEAR SWEATER AND HAT

### SIZE

To fit a bear approx 13¾"/35cm tall.

### GAUGE

18 sts and 22 rows to 4"/10cm over St st and chart pats using larger needles.
TAKE TIME TO CHECK YOUR GAUGE.

### SWEATER—BACK

With A, cast on 37 sts. Work in St st for 2 rows.

### Beg chart 1

**Row 1 (RS)** Work 5 sts A; work next 27 sts in chart pat as foll: work first st of chart, then work 12-st rep twice, work last 2 sts; work 5 sts with A. Cont as established through chart row 26, then cont with A to end of piece, AT SAME TIME, when piece measures 2½"/6.5cm from beg, end with a WS row and work as foll:

### Armhole shaping

Bind off 5 sts at beg of next 2 rows—27 sts. Work even until piece measures 4½"/ 11.5cm from beg, end with a WS row.

### Neck shaping

**Next row (RS)** Work 7 sts, join 2nd ball of yarn and bind off center 13 sts, work to end. Working both sides at once, dec 1 st at each neck edge every other row 3 times. Bind off rem 4 sts each side for shoulders.

*(Continued on page 129)*

# Natural Wonder

## for intermediate knitters

A tweedy cardigan spans the seasons in pint-sized style. A cinch to knit in quick-and-easy garter stitch, this wear-anywhere classic is subtly detailed with simple patch pockets and rolled cuffs. "Natural Wonder" first appeared in the Fall '99 issue of *Family Circle Easy Knitting* magazine.

## MATERIALS

- *Cleckheaton Country 8 Ply Naturals* by Plymouth Yarn, 1³⁄₄oz/50g balls, each approx 110yd/100m (wool/acrylic/nylon)
  3 (4, 5) balls in #1805 natural
- One pair size 5 (3.75mm) needles OR SIZE TO OBTAIN GAUGE
- Four ⁵⁄₈"/15mm buttons
- Stitch holder

## SIZES

Sized for 6 (9, 12)months. Shown in size 6 months.

## FINISHED MEASUREMENTS

- Chest (buttoned) 21¹⁄₂ (23, 24)"/54.5 (58.5, 61)cm
- Length 9¹⁄₂ (10, 11¹⁄₂)"/24 (26, 29)cm
- Upper arm 10 (10¹⁄₄, 11)"/25 (26, 28)cm

## GAUGE

24 sts and 47 rows to 4"/10cm over garter st using size 5 (3.75mm) needles.
TAKE TIME TO CHECK YOUR GAUGE.

## Notes

**1** Cardigan is made in one piece, beg with the two fronts and ending with the back.
**2** Buttonholes are written for the right front. If making cardigan for a boy, work buttonholes on left front.

## LEFT FRONT

Cast on 35 (37, 39) sts. Work in garter st for 4¹⁄₂ (5, 6)"/11.5 (13, 15)cm.

### Sleeve shaping

Cast on at beg of RS rows as foll: 2 sts 8 (6, 4) times, 3 sts 2 (5, 8), 15 sts once—72 (79, 86) sts. Work even until piece measures 8 (8¹⁄₂, 10)"/20 (22, 25)cm from beg, end with a RS row.

### Neck shaping

**Next row (WS)** Bind off 4 (5, 6) sts (neck edge), work to end. Cont to bind off from neck edge 3 sts once, 2 sts once, dec 1 st every other row twice—61 (67, 73) sts. Work even until piece measures 9¹⁄₂ (10, 11¹⁄₂)"/24 (26, 29)cm from beg, end with a WS row. Place sts on a holder. Place markers on front edge for 4 buttons, the first one 1¹⁄₂ (1³⁄₄, 2)"/4 (4.5, 5)cm from lower edge and the other 3 spaced 2 (2¹⁄₄, 2¹⁄₂)"/5 (5.5, 6.5)cm apart.

### RIGHT FRONT

Work to correspond to left front, reversing shaping and working buttonholes opposite markers as foll: At beg of a RS row, k2, bind off 2 sts, work to end. On the foll row, cast on 2 sts over bound-off sts. When piece measures same as left front, keep sts on needle to work next row from RS.

### BACK

**Next row (RS)** Work sts from left front holder, cast on 17 (19, 21) sts for back neck, work sts of right front—139 (153, 167) sts. Cont on all sts until piece measures 12³⁄₄ (13¹⁄₄, 15)"/32.5 (33.5, 38)cm from beg.

### Sleeve shaping

Bind off 15 sts at beg of next 2 rows, 3 sts at beg of next 4 (10, 16) rows, 2 sts at beg of next 16 (12, 8) rows—65 (69, 73) sts. Work even until piece measures 19 (20, 23)"/48 (52, 58)cm. Bind off all sts.

### POCKETS (make 2)

Cast on 18 sts and work in garter st for 2¹⁄₂"/6cm. Bind off.

### FINISHING

Block pieces to measurements.

### Neckband

With RS facing, beg at right front neck, pick up and k 61(65, 69) sts evenly around neck edge. Work in garter st for 4 rows. Bind off. Sew pockets to fronts, 1¹⁄₂"/4cm from lower edge and 1¹⁄₄ (1¹⁄₂, 1³⁄₄)"/3.5 (4, 4.5)cm from side edge. Fold cardigan at shoulders and sew side and sleeve seams. Sew on buttons.

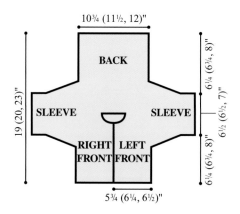

# Play Date

## for beginner knitters

Stitched in a muted mix of heathered tweed stripes, this rough-and-tumble rolled-neck pullover will hold up to whatever your little sport can dish out. "Play Date" first appeared in the Winter '99/'00 issue of *Family Circle Easy Knitting* magazine.

## MATERIALS

- *Fox* by Grignasco/JCA, 1¾oz/50g skeins, each approx 193yd/175m (wool/acrylic)
  3 (3, 4, 5) skeins in #800 ecru (A)
  1 (1, 2, 2) skeins each in #693 grey (B), #488 blue (C) and #489 brown (D)
- One pair each sizes 7 and 9 (4.5 and 5.5mm) needles OR SIZE TO OBTAIN GAUGE
- Size 7 (4.5mm) circular needle 16"/40cm long

## SIZES

Sized for Child's 2 (4, 6, 8). Shown in size 2.

## FINISHED MEASUREMENTS

- Chest 26 (29, 32, 35)"/66 (73.5, 81.5, 89)cm
- Length 13 (14½, 16, 17½)"/33 (37, 41, 44.5)cm
- Upper arm 10 (11, 12, 13)"/25.5 (28, 31.5, 33)cm

## GAUGE

17 sts and 25 rows to 4"/10cm over St st and 2 strands of yarn held tog using larger needles. TAKE TIME TO CHECK YOUR GAUGE.

### Stripe pattern

Color 1 = 2 strands A
Color 2 = 1 strand each A and B
Color 3 = 1 strand each A and C
Color 4 = 1 strand each A and D
*Work 6 rows each Colors 1, 3, 4, 1; work 8 rows Color 2; work 6 rows each Colors 4 and 3; rep from * (44 rows) for stripe pat.

## BACK

With smaller needles and Color 1, cast on 56 (62, 68, 74) sts. Work in k2, p2 rib as foll: 1 row Color 1, 2 rows Color 2, 2 rows Color 1, 4 rows Color 2. Change to larger needles and work in St st and stripe pat until piece measures 8 (9, 10, 11)"/20.5 (23, 25.5, 28)cm from beg, end with a WS row.

### Armhole shaping

Dec 1 st each side on next row, then every other row 5 times more—44 (50, 56, 62) sts. Work even until armhole measures 3½ (4, 4½, 5)"/8.5 (10, 11.5, 12.5)cm, end with a WS row.

### Neck shaping

**Next row (RS)** Work 19 (22, 24, 26) sts, join 2nd ball of yarn and bind off center 6 (6, 8, 10) sts for neck, work to end. Cont working both sides at once, bind off from each neck edge 3 sts once, 2 sts once, dec 1 st every other row twice. Work even until armhole measures 5 (5½, 6, 6½)"/12.5 (14, 15.5, 16.5)cm. Bind off rem 12 (15, 17, 19) sts each side for shoulders.

### FRONT

Work as for back.

### SLEEVES

With smaller needles, cast on 30 (32, 34, 36) sts. Work in k2, p2 rib as for back. Change to larger needles. Work in St st and stripe pat, inc 1 st each side every 6th row 1 (3, 6, 8) times, every 8th row 6 (5, 3, 2) times—44 (48, 52, 56) sts. Work even until piece measures 11 (11½, 12, 12½)"/28 (29, 30.5, 31.5)cm from beg.

### Cap shaping

Work as for back armhole shaping. Bind off rem 32 (36, 40, 44) sts.

### FINISHING

Block pieces to measurements. Sew shoulder seams.

### Neckband

With RS facing, circular needle and Color 1, pick up and k 60 (60, 64, 68) sts evenly around neck edge. Join and work in rnds of k2, p2 rib as foll: 3 rnds Color 1, 2 rnds Color 2, 2 rnds Color 1, 8 rnds Color 2, 2 rnds Color 1, 2 rnds Color 2, 2 rnds Color 1, 2 rnds Color 2 and 2 rnds Color 1. With Color 1, bind off all sts in rib. Set in sleeves. Sew side and sleeve seams.

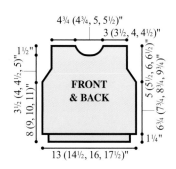

# Bear Necessity

## for intermediate knitters

Get ready to hit the slopes. A tot-sized teddy skis down the front of this cheerful Scandinavian-style pullover. A Fair Isle design decorates the cuffs, shoulder and bottom band; button closures at the shoulders make it easy to put on and take off. "Bear Necessity" first appeared in the Winter '00/'01 issue of *Family Circle Easy Knitting* magazine.

## MATERIALS

- *Knitaly*® by Colorado Yarns, 3½oz/ 100g balls, each approx 215yd/195m (wool)
  3 (3, 4) balls in #2425 ecru (MC)
  1 ball each in #1369 red (A), #2408 brown (B), #25399 green (C), #1415 periwinkle (D),
  #1650 tan (E), #20426 charcoal (F) and #955013 black (G)
- One pair each sizes 4 and 6 (3.5 and 4mm) needles OR SIZE TO OBTAIN GAUGE
- Three 5/8"/15mm buttons
- Two black beads for eyes

## SIZES

Sized for Child's 2 (4, 6). Shown in size 2.

## FINISHED MEASUREMENTS

- Chest 26 (29, 32)"/66 (73.5, 81.5)cm
- Length 13½ (14½, 16)"/34.5 (37, 40.5)cm
- Upper arm 11 (12, 13)"/28 (31, 33)cm

## GAUGE

18 sts and 24 rows to 4"/10cm over St st using larger needles.
TAKE TIME TO CHECK YOUR GAUGE.

## K3, P2 rib

**Row 1 (RS)** *K3, p2; rep from * to end.
**Row 2** K the knit sts and p the purl sts.
Rep row 2 for k3, p2 rib.

## BACK

With smaller needles and A, cast on 60 (65, 70) sts. Change to MC and work in k3, p2 rib for 4 rows, inc 0 (1, 2) sts on last row—60 (66, 72) sts. Change to larger needles and work 11 rows chart 1. Cont in St st with MC only until piece measures 12½ (13½, 15)"/31.5 (34.5, 38)cm from beg.

## Beg chart 2

**Row 1 (RS)** Beg with st 7 (4, 1) work to last st, work 8-st rep 7 times, work sts 1 to 2 (5, 8). Cont in chart as established through row 7. Bind off all sts.

## FRONT

Work as for back until 11 rows of chart 1 have been worked. Cont in St st with MC only for 3 (5, 9) rows.

## Beg chart 3

**Row 1 (RS)** Work 6 (9, 12) sts in St st with MC, work 48 sts chart 3, work 6 (9, 12) sts MC. Cont as established through chart row 47, then work all sts with MC until piece measures 11½ (12½, 13½)"/29.5 (32, 34)cm from beg, end with a WS row.

## Neck shaping

**Next Row (RS)** Work 25 (28, 31) sts, join 2nd ball of yarn and bind off center 10 sts for neck, work to end. Cont working both sides at once, bind off 3 sts from each neck edge once, 2 sts once, dec 1 st every other row 2 (3, 4) times, AT SAME TIME, when piece measures 12½ (13½, 15)"/31.5 (34.5, 38)cm from beg, work 7 rows chart 2 as for back. Bind off rem 18 (20, 22) sts each side for shoulders.

## SLEEVES

With smaller needles and A, cast on 30 (35, 35) sts. Change to MC and work in k3, p2 rib for 4 rows, inc 4 (1, 3) sts on last row—34 (36, 38) sts. Change to larger needles and work 11 rows chart 1, then cont in St st with MC only, AT SAME TIME, inc 1 st each side every 6th row 8 (9, 10) times—50 (54, 58) sts. Work even until piece measures 10 (11, 12½)"/25.5 (28, 31.5)cm from beg. Bind off.

## Bear's scarf

With larger needles and A, cast on 6 sts and work in St st for 6"/15cm. Bind off.

## FINISHING

Block pieces to measurements. Embroider ski poles with chain st and nose with satin st. Knot scarf and sew to bear's neck. Sew on beads for eyes. Sew right shoulder seam.

## Neckband

With RS facing, smaller needles and MC, pick up and k 70 (75, 80) sts and work in k3, p2 rib for 4 rows. Change to A and work in St st for 5 rows. Bind off.

Sew left shoulder seam at 1¼ (1½, 2)"/3 (4, 5)cm from shoulder edge. Make three buttonloops evenly along front shoulder and neckband. Sew buttons to back opposite loops.

Place markers 5½ (6, 6½)"/14 (15.5, 16.5)cm down from shoulder seams on front and back for armholes. Sew top of sleeves between markers. Sew side and sleeve seams.

*(Schematics and charts on page 130)*

# Mad About Blue
## for beginner knitters

Bundle up baby in this cuddly zip-front bouclé jacket accented with subtle Fair Isle patterning and ribbed edging. The matching hat on page 62 makes a stylish companion. "Mad About Blue" first appeared in the Fall '99 issue of *Family Circle Easy Knitting* magazine.

## MATERIALS

- *Soft Bouclé* by Bernat®, 5oz/140g skeins, each approx 255yd/232m (acrylic/polyester)
  2 (2, 3) skeins in #22931 blue (A)
  1 (1, 2) skeins in #6713 white (B)
- One pair each sizes 6 and 8 (4 and 5mm) needles OR SIZE TO OBTAIN GAUGE
- One 10 (12, 12)"/25 (30, 30)cm separating zipper

## SIZES

Sized for Newborn (6, 12) months. Shown in size 6 months.

## FINISHED MEASUREMENTS

- Chest (closed) 27 (29, 30)"/68.5 (73.5, 76)cm
- Length 10¼ (11½, 12½)"/26 (29, 32)cm
- Upper arm 11½ (12½, 13)"/29 (32, 33)cm

## GAUGE

16 sts and 24 rows to 4"/10cm over St st using larger needles.
TAKE TIME TO CHECK YOUR GAUGE.

## BACK

With smaller needles and B, cast on 49 (53, 55) sts. Work in k1, p1 rib for 1¼"/3cm, inc 4 sts evenly across last row—53 (57, 59) sts. Change to larger needles.

### Beg chart pat

**Row 1 (RS)** Beg with st 4 (2, 1), work to st 13, work 10-st rep 4 times, end with st 16 (18, 19). Cont in pat as established through row 20, then cont to rep rows 14-19 until piece measures 9½ (10¾, 11¾)"/24 (27, 30)cm from beg.

### Neck shaping

**Next row (RS)** Work 21 (22, 23) sts, join 2nd ball of yarn and bind off center 11 (13, 13) sts, work to end. Working both sides at once with separate balls of yarn, bind off 2 sts from each neck edge once. When piece measures 10¼ (11½, 12½)"/26 (29, 32)cm from beg, bind off rem 19 (20, 21) sts each side for shoulders.

## LEFT FRONT

With smaller needles and B, cast on 24 (26, 27) sts. Work in k1, p1 rib for 1¼"/3cm, inc 2 sts evenly across last row—26 (28, 29) sts. Change to larger needles.

### Beg chart pat

**Row 1 (RS)** Beg with st 4 (2, 1), work to st 13, work 10-st rep once, end with st 19. Cont in pat as established through row 20, then cont to rep rows 15-20 until piece measures 8¾ (10, 10½)"/22 (25, 27)cm from beg, end with a RS row.

### Neck shaping

**Next row (WS)** Bind off 3 (4, 4) sts (neck edge), work to end. Cont to bind off from neck edge 2 sts once, dec 1 st every other row twice—19 (20, 21) sts. Work even until same length as back. Bind off rem sts for shoulder.

## RIGHT FRONT

Work to correspond to left front, reversing chart pat as foll:

### Beg chart pat

**Row 1 (RS)** Beg with st 1, work to st 13, work 10-st rep once, end with st 16 (18, 19). Reverse neck shaping by working decs at beg of RS rows.

## SLEEVES

With smaller needles and B, cast on 29 (31, 33) sts. Work in k1, p1 rib for 1¼"/3cm, inc 2 sts across last row—31 (33, 35) sts. Change to larger needles.

### Beg chart pat

**Row 1 (RS)** Beg with st 5 (4, 3), work to st 13, work 10-st rep twice, end with st 15 (16, 17). Cont in pat as established through row 9, then cont to rep rows 14-19, AT SAME TIME, inc 1 st each side (working inc sts into pat) every other row 8 (8, 5) times, every 4th row 0 (1, 4) times—47 (51, 53) sts. Work even until piece measures 4½ (5½, 6½)"/11.5 (14, 16.5)cm from beg. Bind off all sts.

## FINISHING

Block pieces to measurements. Sew shoulder seams.

### Neckband

With RS facing, smaller needles and B, pick up and k 55 (59, 63) sts evenly around neck edge. Work in k1, p1 rib for 1"/2.5cm. Bind off in rib.

### Front bands

With RS facing, smaller needles and B, pick up and K 39 (42, 47) sts evenly along each front edge, including side of neckband. K 2 rows. Bind off.
Place markers 5¾ (6¼, 6½)"/14.5 (16, 16.5)cm down from shoulder on front and back. Sew top of sleeves between markers. Sew side and sleeve seams. Sew in zipper. (You may have to shorten zipper to fit.)

*(Schematics and charts on page 130)*

# Baa-Baa Baby

## for beginner knitters

Amy Bahrt's adorable ensemble works up in two shakes of a lamb's tail! The hat knits up in a jiff on circular needles; the matching sweater features a cuddly curly-coated sheep. Both are finished with soft rolled edges. "Baa-Baa Baby" first appeared in the Fall '00 issue of *Family Circle Easy Knitting* magazine.

## MATERIALS

- *Cleckheaton Country 8-ply* by Plymouth Yarn, 1³/₄oz/50g balls, each approx 105yd/96m (wool)
  3 (3, 4) balls in #0288 royal (A)
  2 balls in #2176 green (B) and 1 ball in #2185 caramel (D)
- *Baby Bouclé* by Bernat®, 4oz/113g balls, each approx 204yd/185m (acrylic/polyester)
  1 ball in #101 white (E)
- One pair each sizes 5 and 6 (3.75 and 4mm) needles OR SIZE TO OBTAIN GAUGE
- Size F/5 (4mm) crochet hook
- Bobbins (optional)

## SIZES

Sized for Child's 1 (2, 4). Shown in size 1.

## FINISHED MEASUREMENTS

- Chest 23 (26, 28)"/58 (66, 71)cm
- Length (unrolled) 12¹/₂ (13¹/₂, 14¹/₂)"/31.5 (34, 37)cm
- Upper arm 10 (11, 12)"/25 (28, 30.5)cm
- Hat circumference 16"/40.5cm

## GAUGE

20 sts and 26 rows to 4"/10cm over St st using larger needles.
TAKE TIME TO CHECK YOUR GAUGE.

## Notes

**1** Use a separate ball of yarn for each block of color.
**2** When changing colors, twist yarns tog on WS to prevent holes.
**3** See page 131 for sheep chart

## STRIPE PATTERN

*4 rows A, 4 rows B; rep from * (8 rows) for stripe pat.

## BACK

With larger needles and B, cast on 58 (66 70) sts. Work in St st for 2"/5cm. **Next row** K1 B, *k1 A, k1 B; rep from *, end k2 B. Cont as established for 2 rows more (for grass pat). Then work in St st with A only until piece measures 12¹/₂ (13¹/₂, 14¹/₂)"/31.5 (34, 37)cm from beg. Bind off.

## FRONT

Work as for back through grass pat.
**Beg chart pat** (see page 131)
**Next row (RS)** Work 15 (19, 21) sts A, 28 sts chart pat, 15 (19, 21) sts A. Cont as established through chart row 36. With A, work in St st on all sts until piece measures 10 (11, 12)"/25 (27.5, 30.5)cm from beg, end with a WS row.

## Neck shaping

**Next row (RS)** Work 23 (27, 29), join 2nd ball and bind off center 12 sts, work to end. Working both sides at once, bind off from each neck edge 3 sts once, 2 sts once, then dec 1 st every other row twice. Work even until piece measures 12¹/₂ (13¹/₂, 14¹/₂)"/31.5 (34, 37)cm from beg. Bind off rem 16 (20, 22) sts each side for shoulders.

## SLEEVES

With larger needles and B, cast on 32 sts. Work in St st for 1¹/₂"/4cm. Cont in St st and stripe pat, inc 1 st each side on next row, then every 4th row 2 (0, 2) times, every 6th row 6 (11, 11) times—50 (56, 60) sts. Work even until piece measures 9¹/₂ (13, 14)"/24 (33, 35.5)cm from beg. Bind off.

## FINISHING

Block pieces to measurements.

## LAMB

With A, work French knot for eyes. With crochet hook and D, ch 8. Join with sl st to first ch. Sew center tog to close ear. Sew ears to body (see chart for placement).

## Neckband

Sew left shoulder seam. With RS facing, smaller needles and A, pick up and k 72 sts evenly around neck edge. Work in k1, p1 rib for 1"/2.5cm. Work in St st for 1"/2.5cm. Bind off. Sew other shoulder and neckband seam. Place markers 5 (5¹/₂, 6)"/12.5 (14, 15)cm down from shoulders on front and back. Sew sleeves between markers. Sew side and sleeve seams.

## HAT

With larger needles and B, cast on 80 sts. Work in St st for 1¹/₂"/4cm. Cont in St st and stripe pat until piece measures 5¹/₂"/14cm from beg. **Next dec row (RS)** *K6, k2tog; rep from * to end—70 sts. P 1 row. **Next dec row (RS)** *K5, k2tog; rep from * to end—60 sts. P 1 row. **Next dec row (RS)** *K4, k2tog; rep from * to end—50 sts. P 1 row. **Next dec row (RS)** *K3, k2tog; rep from * to end—40 sts. P 1 row. **Next dec row (RS)** K2tog across. Draw yarn through rem 20 sts and pull tightly to close. Sew back seam.

*(Schematics and chart on page 131)*

# The Big Top
## for beginner knitters

Have a little circus fun with this colorful creation from Agi Revesz. An intarsia elephant with dimensional details tosses cheerful circus rings skyward on a simple stockinette-stitch pullover. "The Big Top" first appeared in the Winter '96/'97 issue of *Family Circle Knitting* magazine.

### MATERIALS

- *Utopia* by Unger/JCA 3¹/₂oz/100g skeins each approx 240yd/216m (acrylic)

  2 (2, 3, 3) skeins in #126 navy (MC)

  1 skein in #278 chartreuse (CC)

  1 skein each in #4301 purple (A), #1001 white (B), #2298 canary (C), #2332 orange (D), #4089 magenta (E), #7162 royal (F) and #6186 seafoam (G)
- Embroidery Floss by J&P Coats each skein approx 9yd/8m (cotton)
- One pair each sizes 6 and 7 (4 and 4.5mm) needles OR SIZE TO OBTAIN GAUGE
- Size 5 (1.75mm) steel crochet hook
- Embroidery needle

### SIZES

To fit sizes 18 mo (2, 3, 4). Shown in size 4.

### FINISHED MEASUREMENTS

- Chest at underarm 24 (26, 28, 30)"/61 (66, 71, 76)cm
- Length 13 (14, 15, 16)"/33 (35.5, 38, 40.5)cm
- Width at upperarm 11 (12, 12¹/₂, 13)"/28 (30.5, 32, 33)cm

### GAUGE

18 sts and 28 rows to 4"/10cm over St st using size 7 (4.5mm) needles
TAKE TIME TO CHECK YOUR GAUGE.

### Note

When changing colors, twist yarns on WS to prevent holes. Use bobbins for colorwork.

### BACK

With smaller needles and MC, cast on 54 (60, 64, 68) sts. Work in k2, p2 rib for 1"/2.5cm, end with a WS row. Change to larger needles. Work in St st until piece measures 13 (14, 15, 16)"/33 (35.5, 38, 40.5)cm from beg. Bind off.

### FRONT

Work as for back until piece measures 3 (3, 3¹/₂, 3¹/₂)"/7.5 (7.5, 9, 9)cm from beg, end with a WS row. **Next row (RS)** Work first 13 (16, 18, 20) sts then beg chart with CC. After completing chart, cont in pat as established until piece measures 11 (12, 13, 14)"/28 (30.5, 33, 35.5)cm from beg, end with a WS row.

### Neck shaping

**Next row (RS)** Work 24 (27, 29, 30) sts, join 2nd ball of yarn and bind off 6 (6, 6, 8) sts, work to end. Working both sides at once, bind off from each neck edge 3 sts once then 2 sts once. Dec 1 st each neck edge 2 (2, 2, 3) times—17 (20, 22, 22) sts. Work even until piece measures same as back. Bind off.

### SLEEVES

With smaller needles and MC, cast on 28 (30, 32, 32) sts. Work in k2, p2 rib for 1"/2.5cm, end with a WS row. Change to larger needles, work in St st and AT SAME TIME, inc 1 st each side every 4th row 8 (7, 6, 3) times and every 6th row 3 (5, 6, 11) times—50 (54, 56, 60) sts. Work even until piece measures 9 (10, 11, 12)"/23 (25.5, 28, 30.5)cm from beg. Bind off.

### FINISHING

### Ear

With larger needles and CC, cast on 3 sts. Work 2 rows in St st, then inc 1 st each side, every row 3 times—9 sts. Work 3 rows more. Bind off.

### Blanket

Holding 2 strands of A tog, with smaller needles, cast on 10 sts. Work in garter st for 16 rows. Bind off.

### Ring

(Make one ring each of the foll colors: C, D, E, F, G) Holding 2 strands tog, with crochet hook, ch 15, join with a sl st to form a ring, ch 1. Work 2 sc in each ch, join with a sl st. Leaving a tail to sew on, fasten off. Sew ear and rings in place on front as pictured. With MC embroider eye with French knots and backstitch leg details. With 2 strands of B work satin st for tusk and with C edge st around blanket edges. Chain st tail with CC. Block all pieces to measurements. Sew right shoulder seam.

### Neckband

With RS facing, smaller needles and MC, beg at right front neck, pick up and k 52 (54, 54, 58) sts evenly around neck edge. Work 12 rows in k2, p2 rib. Bind off loosely in rib. Sew left shoulder and neckband seam. Fold neck rib to inside and sew in place. Mark 5¹/₂ (6, 6¹/₄, 6¹/₂)"/14 (15, 16, 16.5)cm down sides from shoulders for armholes. Sew sleeves between markers. Sew side and sleeve seams.

*(Schematics and chart on page 131)*

# Bits and Pieces

Chill-chasing accessories outfit your wee one head to toe for every occasion.

Beguiling booties with rollover cuffs are garter stitched in a tweedy yarn—a perfect project for beginning knitters. Pair with the matching cardigan on page 46 for a great shower gift. "First Steps" first appeared in the Fall '99 issue of *Family Circle Easy Knitting* magazine.

## MATERIALS

- *Cleckheaton Country 8 Ply Naturals* by Plymouth Yarn, 1³⁄₄oz/50g balls, each approx 110yd/100m (wool/acrylic/nylon)
  1 ball in #1805 natural
- One pair size 5 (3.75mm) needles OR SIZE TO OBTAIN GAUGE
- Stitch holders

## SIZES

Sized for Newborn (3, 6) months. Shown in size 3 months.

## GAUGE

24 sts and 47 rows to 4"/10cm over garter st using size 5 (3.75mm) needles.
TAKE TIME TO CHECK YOUR GAUGE.

## CUFF

Cast on 15 sts and work in garter st for 5 (5³⁄₄, 6¹⁄₂)"/13 (14.5, 16.5)cm. Bind off. Along one long side, pick up and k 30 (34, 38) sts and work in garter st for 10 (12, 14) rows. Cut yarn.

### Instep

**Next row (RS)** Place first and last 10 (12, 14) sts on a holder and work 11 (13, 13) rows in garter st on center 10 sts. Cut yarn. **Next row (RS)** Work 10 (12, 14) sts from right holder, pick up and k 7 (8, 9) sts along side of instep, work center 10 sts on needle, pick up and k 7 (8, 9) sts along other side of instep, work 10 (12, 14) sts from left holder—44 (50, 56) sts. K next row, inc 1 st each side of center 10 sts—46 (52, 58) sts. Cont in garter st for 10 (12, 14) rows.

### Sole

**Next row (RS)** K3 (4, 5), SK2P, k11 (12, 13), k3 tog, k6 (8, 10), SK2P, k11 (12, 13), k3tog, k3 (4, 5)—38 (44, 50) sts. K 1 row.

**Next row (RS)** K2 (3, 4), SK2P, k9 (10, 11), k3 tog, k4 (6, 8), SK2P, k9 (10, 11), k3tog, k2 (3, 4)—30 (36, 42) sts. K 1 row.

**Next row (RS)** K1 (2, 3), SK2P, k7 (8, 9), k3 tog, k2 (4, 6), SK2P, k7 (8, 9), k3tog, k1 (2, 3)—22 (28, 34) sts.

### For size 6 months only

K 1 row. Next row K2, SK2P, k7, k3tog, k4, SK2P, k7, k3tog, k2—26 sts.

### For all sizes

K 2 rows. Divide sts on two needles and weave sts tog. Sew back seam, reversing seam at cuff.

This warm wooly cap is a favorite winter warmer. Adorned with pompoms, this fuzzy flecked number is made to match the cozy jacket on page 52. "Hats Off" first appeared in the Fall '99 issue of *Family Circle Easy Knitting* magazine.

## MATERIALS

- *Soft Bouclé* by Bernat®, 5oz/140g skeins, each approx 255yd/232m (wool/polyamide) 1 skein each in #22931 blue (A) and #6713 white (B)
- One pair each sizes 6 and 8 (4 and 5mm) needles OR SIZE TO OBTAIN GAUGE

## SIZES

Sized for Newborn (6, 12) months. Shown in size 6 months.

## FINISHED MEASUREMENTS

- Head circumference 14½ (15½, 16½)"/37 (39.5, 42)cm

## GAUGE

16 sts and 24 rows to 4"/10cm over St st using larger needles.
TAKE TIME TO CHECK YOUR GAUGE.

## HAT

With smaller needles and A, cast on 55 (59, 63) sts. Work in k1, p1 rib for 1¼"/3cm, inc 4 sts evenly across last row—59 (63, 67) sts. Change to larger needles.

### Beg chart pat

**Next row (RS)** Beg with st 1 (4, 2), work to beg of rep, work 10-st rep 5 (6, 6) times, end with st 19 (16, 18). Cont in pat as established through row 9, then cont to rep rows 14-19 until piece measures 10½ (11, 11½)"/27 (28, 29)cm from beg. Bind off.

### FINISHING

Block piece. Fold piece in half widthwise and sew side and top seam. With B, make two 1½"/4cm pompoms and sew to each corner at top of hat.

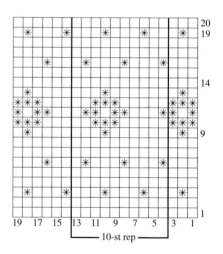

**Color Key**
☐ Blue (A)
✳ White (B)

Wrap it up! A pompom-trimmed garter-stitched scarf and matching mittens are easy-to-make gifts—they're sure-to-be treasured by mom and her little one. "Winter Warmers" first appeared in the Fall '99 issue of *Family Circle Easy Knitting* magazine.

## MATERIALS

- *Kroy 4 Ply* by Patons®, 1³⁄₄oz/50g balls, each approx 203yd/186m (wool/nylon)
  2 skeins in #461 ecru (MC)
  1 skein in #495 tan (CC)
- One pair size 3 (3mm) needles OR SIZE TO OBTAIN GAUGE
- Stitch holders

## SIZES

Sized for Newborn/6 (12/18) months. Shown in size Newborn/6 months.

## GAUGE

28 sts and 52 rows to 4"/10cm over garter st using size 3 (3mm) needles.
TAKE TIME TO CHECK YOUR GAUGE.

## SCARF

With MC, cast on 28 sts and work in garter st for 25¹⁄₂"/65cm. Bind off. With CC, make four 1"/2.5cm pompoms and sew to corners at each end.

## MITTENS

## RIGHT MITTEN

With MC, cast on 34 (38) sts. Work in k2, p2 rib for 2¹⁄₂"/6cm. Work in garter st, dec 2 sts on first row—32 (36) sts. Work even until piece measures 3 (3¹⁄₄)"/8 (8.5)cm from beg. Work first 5 sts and slip to a holder for thumb. Cast on 5 sts and work even until piece measures 4¹⁄₄ (4¹⁄₂)"/10.5 (11.5)cm from beg.

### Top shaping

**Next row (RS)** K3, k2tog, k7 (9), SKP, k4, k2tog, k7 (9), SKP, k3—28 (32) sts. K 1 row.

**Next row (RS)** K3, k2tog, k5 (7), SKP, k4, k2tog, k5 (7), SKP, k3—24 (28) sts. K 1 row.

**Next row (RS)** K3, k2tog, k3 (5), SKP, k4, k2tog, k3 (5), SKP, k3—20 (24) sts. K 1 row.

**Next row (RS)** K3, k2tog, k1 (3), SKP, k4, k2tog, k1 (3), SKP, k3—16 (20) sts. K 1 row.

**Next row (RS)** K2 (3), k2tog, k0 (1), SKP, k4, k2tog, k0 (1), SKP, k2 (3)—12 (16) sts. K 1 row.

*For size 12/18 months only*
**Next row** K2, k2tog, SKP, k4, k2tog, SKP, k2—12 sts. K 1 row.

**For both sizes**
Bind off all sts.

### Thumb

Sl 5 sts from holder to needle, pick up and k 5 sts over cast-on sts, inc 0 (1) st—10 (11) sts. Work in garter st for 10 (12) rows. K2tog across next row. Cut yarn and draw through rem sts.

## LEFT MITTEN

Work to correspond to right hand, reversing placement of thumb, by placing 5 sts on holder at end of first row above rib.

## FINISHING

Sew back and thumb seam.

Lila Chin's flower-accented bibs make mealtime special. Trimmed with garter stitch and a single-button closure, these knits stitch up quick in easy stockinette. "Budding Beauties" first appeared in the Spring/Summer '01 issue of *Family Circle Easy Knitting* magazine.

## MATERIALS

- *Windsurf* by Sesia/Colorado Yarns, 1³⁄₄oz/50g balls, each approx 150yd/108m (cotton)
  1 ball each in #99 yellow and #68 pink
- One pair size 3 (3mm) needles OR SIZE TO OBTAIN GAUGE
- 1 decorative button
- 2 small crochet flower appliques

## FINISHED MEASUREMENTS

- Approx 8"/20.5cm by 10"/25.5cm

## GAUGE

26 sts and 35 rows to 4"/10cm over St st using size 3 (3mm) needles.

TAKE TIME TO CHECK YOUR GAUGE.

## BIB

With color chosen, cast on 30 sts. Work in St st, inc 1 st each side every other row 11 times—52 sts. Work even until piece measures 5¹⁄₂"/14cm, end with a WS row.

**Neck shaping**

**Next row (RS)** K18 and place sts on a holder for left front, join 2nd ball of yarn and bind off center 16 sts, k to end. Working on right front sts only and cont in St st, work 1 row even.

**Next row (RS)** K1, ssk, k to end.

**Next row (WS)** P to last 3 sts, p2tog tbl, p1. Rep last 2 rows until 12 sts rem. Work even for 13 rows. Inc 1 st at the beg of every RS row 3 times—15 sts.

**Next row (RS)** Inc 1 st, k to last 3 sts, k3tog. Work 1 row even.

Rep last 2 rows until 8 sts rem. Bind off.

Sl sts from holder to needle and work left front to correspond to right front, reversing shaping as foll: For neck dec, on RS rows, work to last 3 sts, k2tog, k1; on WS rows, p1, p2tog, p to end.

Work inc sts at end of RS rows and dec 2 sts at beg of RS rows. Cont as established until 10 sts rem.

**Next (buttonhole) row (RS)** Dec 2 sts, k2, yo, k2tog, k2, inc 1—9 sts. Work 3 rows even, then bind off.

## FINISHING

With RS facing, circular needle and CC, beg at upper left hand tab, pick up and k 244 sts evenly around outside edge of bib. Join and work in rev St st (p every rnd) for 3 rnds. Bind off. Block lightly. Sew 1 flower applique in each corner at lower edge (see photo). Sew on button.

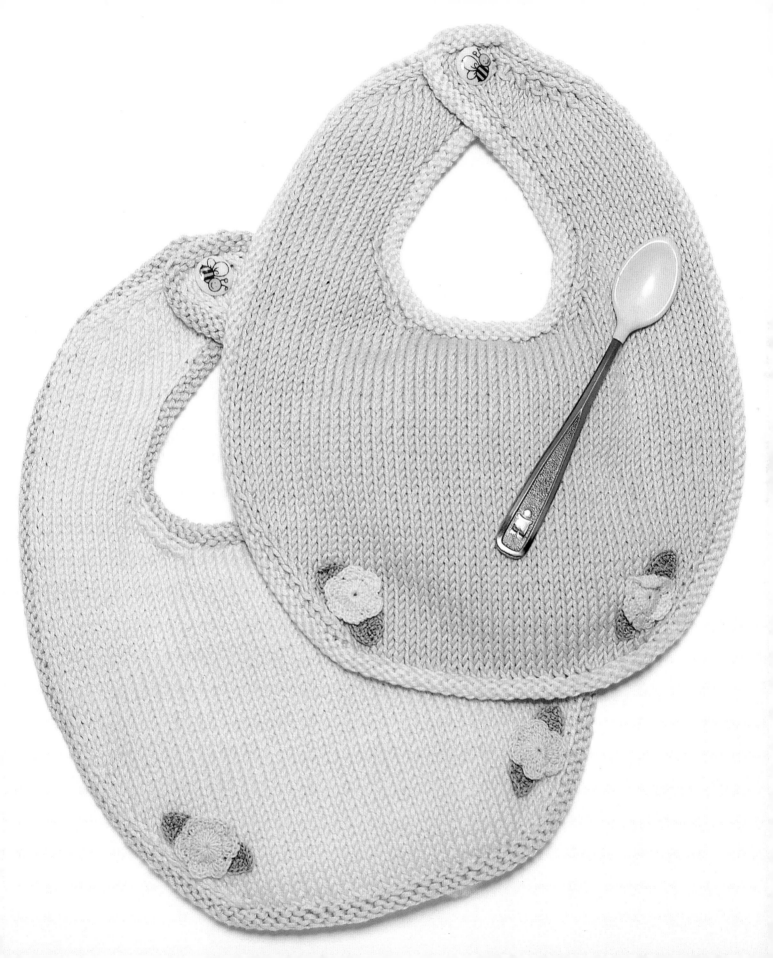

Everywhere that baby goes, this sheepy tote is sure to follow. Amy Bahrt's striped stockinette diaper bag has room for bottles, wipes, toys and more. It's the perfect companion piece to the cozy sweater (page 54), blanket (page 82) and pillows (page 84). "Wool Gathering" first appeared in the Fall '00 issue of *Family Circle Easy Knitting* magazine.

## MATERIALS

■ *Cleckheaton Country 8-Ply* by Plymouth Yarn, 1³⁄₄oz/50g balls, each approx 105yd/96m (wool)
   5 balls each #2176 green (B)
   1 ball each in #0288 royal (A) and #2185 caramel (D)
■ *Baby Bouclé* by Bernat®, 4oz/113g balls, each approx 204yd/185m (wool)
   1 ball in #101 white (E)
■ One pair size 6 (4mm) needles OR SIZE TO OBTAIN GAUGE
■ Size F/5 (4mm) crochet hook
■ Four ⁵⁄₈"/15mm buttons
■ Bobbins (optional)
■ ³⁄₄yd/.7m iron-on interfacing
■ ³⁄₄yd/.7m lining

## FINISHED MEASUREMENTS

■ Approx 12" x 16" x 3"/30.5cm x 40.5cm x 7.5cm

## GAUGE

20 sts and 26 rows to 4"/10cm over St st using size 6 (4mm) needles.
TAKE TIME TO CHECK YOUR GAUGE.

### Notes

**1** Use a separate ball of yarn for each block of color.
**2** When changing colors, twist yarns tog on WS to prevent holes.
**3** Bag is made in one piece, beg at back and worked to front with both sides picked up and worked separately.

## DIAPER BAG

With B, cast on 80 sts for top of back piece. Work in St st for 1¹⁄₂"/4cm, end with a RS row. K next row on WS for turning ridge. Cont in St st until piece measures 13¹⁄₂"/34cm from turning ridge,

end with a RS row. K next row on WS for ridge. Cont in St st for 3"/7.5cm more for bottom piece, end with RS row. K next row on WS for ridge. Cont in St st for 7 rows more. Work 4 rows A, 4 rows B, 4 rows A.

### Beg chart pat

Work 26 sts A, 28 sts chart pat, 26 sts A. Cont as established through row 36 of chart. With B, work in St st on all sts until piece measures 12"/30cm from last ridge, end with a RS row. K next row on WS for turning ridge. Cont in St st for 1¹⁄₂"/4cm more. Bind off.

### Sides

With RS facing and B, pick up 16 sts on one side of 3"/7.5cm bottom. Work in St st as foll: 7 rows B, *4 rows A, 4 rows B; rep from * 7 times more, 4 rows A, 1 row B. With B, k next row on WS for ridge. Cont in St st with B for 1¹⁄₂"/4cm more. Bind off.

### Straps (make 2)

With B, cast on 12 sts. Work in St st for 20"/51cm. Bind off.

## FINISHING

Block pieces to measurements.

### Lamb

With A, work French knot for eyes. With crochet hook and D, ch 8. Join with sl st to first ch. Sew center tog to close ear. Sew ears to head (see chart for placement).

Cut interfacing to fit bag. Pin in place and carefully iron on foll manufacturer's instructions. Sew sides to front and back. Fold at turning ridge and sew hem in place.

Cut interfacing to fit strap. Pin in place and carefully iron on foll manufacturer's instructions. Sew side seam. Sew ends closed. Sew straps to inside of bag 5¹⁄₄"/13.5cm from sides.

Cut lining to fit bag. Sew lining and place inside of bag and sl st lining to bag.

Sew buttons on outside of bag through all thicknesses.

*(See chart on page 131)*

Chunky stitches and a simple shape make this colorful stockinette-stitched cap a breeze to stitch. Top it off with an oversized saffron pompom and enjoy the smiles. "Head Start" first appeared in the Fall '01 issue of *Family Circle Easy Knitting* magazine.

## MATERIALS
■ *Primo* by Filatura Di Crosa/Tahki•Stacy Charles, Inc., 1¾oz/50g balls, each approx 81yd/74m (wool)
  2 (2, 2) balls #217 pink (MC)
  1 (1, 1) ball #287 mustard (CC)
■ One pair each sizes 7 and 9 (4.5 and 5.5mm) needles OR SIZE TO OBTAIN GAUGE

## SIZES
Sized for 3-6 months (9-12 months, 18 months). Shown in size 9-12 months.

## GAUGE
16 sts and 24 rows to 4"/10cm over St st using larger needles.
TAKE TIME TO CHECK YOUR GAUGE.

## TOP
With larger needles and MC, cast on 28 (30, 32) sts. Work in St st for 7 (7½, 8)"/18 (19, 20)cm. Bind off.

### Sides
With RS facing, larger needles and MC, pick up and k 28 (30, 32) sts along one side edge.
**Next row (WS)** Purl.
**Next row** K1, SKP, k to last 3 sts, k2tog, k1. Rep last 2 rows 6 times more. Change to smaller needles and work in k1, p1 rib for ¾"/2cm. Bind off in rib. Work in same way along other 3 sides.

## FINISHING
Sew 4 seams. With CC, make four pompoms and sew to each corner (see photo).

# Panda Hat
## for beginner knitters

Hats off to Jean Guirguis's delightful panda hat with pop-out ears. Sure to generate compliments, it makes a terrific topper for your tiny tot. "Panda Hat" first appeared in the Fall '02 issue of *Family Circle Easy Knitting* magazine.

### MATERIALS

■ *Plush* by Berroco, Inc., 1³/₄oz/50g balls, each approx 90yd/83m (nylon)
  1 ball each in #1901 cream (A) and #1934 black (B)
■ One pair each sizes 7 and 9 (4.5 and 5.5mm) needles OR SIZE TO OBTAIN GAUGE
■ 1 pair button eyes
■ Stitch holders

### SIZES

Sized for 1 year.

### FINISHED MEASUREMENTS

■ Head circumference 18"/45.5cm

### GAUGE

20 sts and 16 rows to 4"/10cm over St st using 2 strands of yarn and size 9 (5.5mm) needles. TAKE TIME TO CHECK YOUR GAUGE.

### Notes

**1** Work with 2 strands of yarn held together throughout.
**2** When changing colors, twist yarns on WS to prevent holes.

### FRONT

With smaller needles and 2 strands A, cast on 27 sts. Work in k1, p1 rib for 1"/2.5cm. Change to larger needles. Work in St st for 2¹/₂"/6.5cm.

**Beg chart**

**Next row (RS)** Work 4 sts, work 19 sts of chart, work to end. Cont as established until 12 rows of chart have been worked, AT SAME TIME, when piece measures 5¹/₂"/14cm from beg, dec 1 st each side every other row 3 times as foll: SSK, work to last 2 sts, k2tog—21 sts.

**Shape ears**

**Next row (RS)** Place 7 sts on holder for ear, join a 2nd ball of yarn and bind off center 7 sts, place rem 7 sts on 2nd holder for 2nd ear. With B, pick up and k sts from first holder. Work in St st for 2"/5cm. Bind off. Rep for 2nd ear.

### BACK

Work as for front, omitting chart.

### FINISHING

Sew sides, top and ear seams. Sew on eyes. Embroider nose with B using straight sts (see photo).

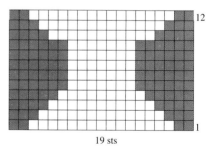

19 sts

**Color Key**

☐ Cream (A)
■ Black (B)

# Snazzy Striped Hat

for intermediate knitters

Nicky Epstein's funky Peruvian hat boasts garter stripes, floppy ear flaps and a knotted I-cord top. "Snazzy Striped Hat" first appeared in the Fall '02 issue of *Family Circle Easy Knitting* magazine.

## MATERIALS

- *1824 Cotton* by Mission Falls/Unique Kolours, 1³⁄₄oz/50g balls, each approx 84yd/77m (cotton) 1 ball each in #305 teal (A), #201 coral (B), #204 gold (C), #302 olive (D), #203 magenta (E) and #404 navy (F)
- One pair size 6 (4mm) needles OR SIZE TO OBTAIN GAUGE
- 1 set (5) dpn size 5 (3.75mm)

## SIZES

Sized for 1-2 years.

## FINISHED MEASUREMENTS

- Head circumference 18"/45.5cm

## GAUGE

19 sts and 23 rows to 4"/10cm over St st using size 6 (4mm) needles.
TAKE TIME TO CHECK YOUR GAUGE.

## STRIPE PATTERN

*4 rows each: A, B, C, D, E, F; rep from * (24 rows) for stripe pat.

### Ear Flaps

(make 2)
With A, cast on 9 sts. Work in garter st and stripe pat, inc 1 st each side every other RS row 3 times—15 sts. Work even until there are 48 rows from beg. Leave both flaps on needle.

### Crown

On same needle with flaps, with A, cast on 14 sts, k across 15 sts of first flap, cast on 28 sts, k across 15 sts of 2nd flap, cast on 14 sts—86 sts. K 3 rows. Cont in stripe pat, dec 10 sts evenly across first row of next E stripe—76 sts. Cont in pat, dec 10 sts evenly across first row of next A stripe—66 sts. Cont in pat, dec 10 sts evenly across first row of next C stripe—56 sts. Cont in pat, dec 10 sts evenly across first row of next—46 sts. K 3 rows. Dec 10 sts evenly across next row—36 sts. K 3 rows.

**Next row** *K2tog; rep from * to end—18 sts. K 1 row.

**Next row** *K2tog; rep from * to end—9 sts. K 1 row.

**Next row** *K2tog; rep from * end k1—5 sts. Change to dpn. P2tog, p1, p2tog—3 sts.

### I cord

*Slide sts to right end of needle and p3. Do not turn work. Rep from * for 4¹⁄₂"/11.5cm. Bind off.

## FINISHING

Sew back seam. Tie I-cord in a knot.

Designed by Annie Modesitt, this circus-inspired hat boasts loop after loop of variegated ribbons just right for your little ringmaster. "Loop Dreams" first appeared in the Fall '02 issue of *Family Circle Easy Knitting* magazine.

## MATERIALS

- *Waterspun* by Classic Elite Yarns, 1¾oz/50g balls, each approx 137yd/123m (wool)
  1 (1, 2, 2) balls in #2532 white (A)
- *Rainbow* by Mokuba Ribbon Company
  50yd/46m #6 rainbow (B)
- One set (4) dpn size 7 (4.5mm) needles OR SIZE TO OBTAIN GAUGE

## SIZES

Sized for 6 months (1, 2, 3-4) years. Shown in size 1.

## FINISHED MEASUREMENTS

- Head circumference 17 (18, 19, 20)"/43 (45.5, 48, 51) cm.

## GAUGE

16 sts and 24 rows to 4"/10cm over st pat using size 7 (4.5mm) needles.
TAKE TIME TO CHECK YOUR GAUGE.

## STITCH GLOSSARY

### Make Loop (ML)

**Rnd 1 (RS)** Insert RH needle into next st on LH needle. Wrap both strands around RH needle, and while the RH needle is still inserted in the stitch, wrap only the ribbon 3 times around the RH needle.

**Next rnd** Only the wool strand and one strand of the ribbon are purled, the rest of the ribbon is pulled off the needle and held to the front of the work.

## HAT

### Garter loop band

With 1 strand each A & B, cast on 68 (72, 76, 80) sts. Divide sts evenly over 3 needles. Join, taking care not to twist sts. Place marker for end of rnd and sl marker every rnd.

**Rnd 1** *K3, ML; rep from * around.

**Rnds 2 and 4** Purl, working the looped stitches by purling only the wool strand and one strand of ribbon, pulling the rest of the ribbon through to the front of the work.

**Rnd 3** *K1, ML, k1; rep from * around.

### Side band

**Next rnd** With A only, *k4, yo; rep from * around—85 (90, 95, 100) sts. Cont in St st until side band measures 2½ (2½, 2¾, 3¼)"/6 (6, 7, 8)cm from end of garter section.

**Next rnd** With 1 strand each of A and B, *k3, k2tog; rep from * to marker—68 (72, 76, 80) sts. Work rnds 1-4 of garter loop band, dec 2 (0, inc 2, inc 4) sts evenly across last rnd—66 (72, 78, 84) sts.

### Shape Top

**Next rnd** With A only, *k11 (12, 13, 14), pm; rep from * around.

**Next rnd** *SSk, k to next marker; rep from * around.

**Next rnd** Knit. Rep last 2 rnds 10 (11, 12, 13) times—6 sts. Cut yarn, leaving a 12½"/31.5cm tail and pull through rem sts on needle.

With a darning needle, weave a single strand of B from the center top of hat to the garter loop band through the 6 ladders created where the stitch markers lay. With a needle and thread stitch the ends of the ribbon tog inside the hat and stitch in place securely, turning ends under to avoid ravelling of ribbon.

Secure this ribbon to the inside back of the hat in the same way.

## HAT BOTTOM

Choose which side of the hat should be the front. Mark the center front with a piece of waste yarn. Place two safety pins 2½ (2½, 2¾, 3¼)"/6 (6, 7, 8)cm from the center front on either side marking a 5 (5, 5½, 6¼)"/12.5 (12.5, 14, 16)cm face opening. Beg at one pin and working around the back of the hat, with a single strand of A, pick up 55 (59, 59, 63) sts to next safety pin.

**Next row (WS)** With a strand of A and B, k5, then with a strand of A only p1, *k1, p1; rep from * across row to last 5 sts, add a strand of B and k 5 sts. Cont working 5 sts each side in garter st using a strand of each A & B and working the center 45 (49, 49, 53) sts in k1, p1 ribbing with A only, until piece measures 2¾ (3, 3, 3¼)"/7 (7.5, 7.5, 8)cm from picked up edge, end with a WS Row. **Next 6 rows** With a strand each of A and B, knit. Bind off all sts.

### Twisted cord

Measure a 24"/61cm length of B and a 48"/122cm length of A. Double the strand of A and fold in half and pull B through the loop created at the center point of the doubled A strand so that A and B are joined at the midpoint where the two different fibers meet. You will have a 48"/122cm length of untwisted strands, from the midpoint

*(Continued on page 132)*

# Cab Fare

for intermediate knitters

Amy Bahrt's charming taxicab hat is highlighted with subtle stripes and a ribbed hem. Black and white buttons make clever little wheels. "Cab Fare" first featured in the Fall '02 issue of *Family Circle Easy Knitting* magazine.

## MATERIALS

- *Cotton Classic II* by Tahki•Stacy Charles, Inc., 1¾ oz/50g, each approx 74yd/68m (cotton)
  1 ball each #2001 white (A), #2997 red (B), #2744 green (C); #2924 purple (D),
  #2533 yellow (E) and #2002 black (F)
- Eight ½"/13mm black and white buttons
- One pair each sizes 5 and 7 (3.75 and 4.5mm) needles OR SIZE TO OBTAIN GAUGE
- Size E/4 (3.5mm) crochet hook

## SIZES

Sized for 1 year (2 years). Shown in size 1 year.

## FINISHED MEASUREMENTS

- Head circumference 16 (18)"/40.5 (45.5)cm

## GAUGE

20 sts and 24 rows to 4"/10cm over St st and chart pats using larger needles.
TAKE TIME TO CHECK YOUR GAUGE.

## STRIPE PATTERN

Working in St st, work 2 rows C, 4 rows D, 2 rows E, 4 rows D, work with C to end of hat.

## HAT

With smaller needles and D, cast on 79 (91) sts. Work in k1, p1 rib for 7 rows. Change to larger needles and St st as foll: 4 rows with C, 1 row with D.

**Beg charts**

**Next row (RS)** *K6 (5) with D, work 12 sts taxi chart; rep from * to last 7 (6) sts, k7 (6) with D.

Cont as established until 10 rows of charts have been worked. Change to D and work 3 rows even. Then work in stripe pat, AT SAME TIME, shape crown.

**Crown shaping**

Work in stripe pat as foll: **Next (dec) row (RS)** *K9, k2tog; rep from * to last 2 (3) sts, k2 (3)—72 (83) sts. Work 1 row even.

**Next (dec) row (RS)** *K8, k2tog; rep from * to last 2 (3) sts, k2 (3)—65 (75) sts. Work 1 row even. Cont to dec 7 (8) sts in this way every other row 5 (6) times more—30 (27) sts, end with a WS row.

**Next row (RS)** *K2tog; rep from *, end k0 (1). Cut off yarn and pull through rem 15 (14) sts. Draw up and fasten securely.

## FINISHING

Sew back seam. Sew on buttons as indicated on chart.

**Taxi Chart**

12 sts

**Color Key**

- ⊡ White (A)
- ☐ Red (B)
- ■ Green (C)
- ⊞ Purple (D)
- ☒ Yellow (E)
- ☑ Black (F)
- ⊗ Wheel (button) placement
- • French knot with A

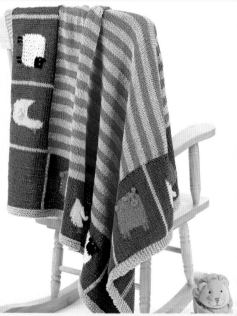

# Cradle Comfort

Beautiful blankets bring sweet dreams.

# Counting Sheep
## for beginner knitters

Worked in a wooly yarn to keep your wee one toasty warm, this stockinette patchwork afghan designed by Amy Bahrt has a garter-stitch border and sheep motifs with fleece as white as snow. "Counting Sheep" first appeared in the Fall '00 issue of *Family Circle Easy Knitting* magazine.

### MATERIALS

- *Cleckheaton Country 8-ply* by Plymouth Yarn, 1¾oz/50g balls, each approx 105yd/96m (wool)
  - 4 balls each in #0288 royal (A) and #2176 green (B)
  - 3 balls in #2178 red (C)
  - 1 ball in #2185 caramel (D)
- *Baby Bouclé* by Bernat®, 4oz/113g balls, each approx 204yd/185m (acrylic/polyester)
  - 1 ball in #1890 white (E)
- One pair size 6 (4mm) needles OR SIZE TO OBTAIN GAUGE
- Size F/5 (4mm) crochet hook
- Bobbins (optional)

### FINISHED MEASUREMENTS

- Approx 27" x 36"/68.5cm x 91cm

### GAUGE

20 sts and 26 rows to 4"/10cm over St st using size 6 (4mm) needles.
TAKE TIME TO CHECK YOUR GAUGE.

### Notes

**1** Blanket is worked in one piece or it may be worked in 4 separate strips and sewn tog.
**2** Use a separate ball of yarn for each block of color. Use a separate ball/bobbin of B for garter st edges.
**3** When changing colors, twist yarns tog on WS to prevent holes.

### AFGHAN

Cast on 5 sts B, 32 sts A, 32 sts C, 32 sts A, 32 sts B, 5 sts B—138 sts. Keeping the first and last 5 sts in garter st in B, work blocks in St st foll diagram for color and chart pat (each block is 32 sts and 36 rows). Bind off.

### FINISHING

Block afghan. With RS facing and B, pick up 138 sts evenly along top and bottom edge. Work in garter st for 8 rows. Bind off.

### LAMB

With A, work a French knot for eyes. With crochet hook and D, ch 8. Join with sl st to first ch. Sew center tog to close ear. See chart.

**PLACEMENT DIAGRAM**

| B | A | C | A |
|---|---|---|---|
| A | C | A | B |
| C | A | B | C |
| A | B | C | A |
| C | A | B | C |
| A | C | A | B |

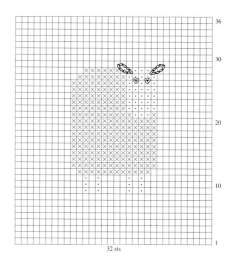

32 sts

### Color Key

- ☐ Background color (MC)
- ♉ French knot with Blue (A)
- · Gold (C)
- ☒ White (B)
- ∅ Chain st with Gold (D)

Worked in saturated hues, Amy Bahrt's snuggly-soft pillows are lofty accents for the nursery. Easy stockinette stitches make for a speedy finish; complement them with the matching afghan on page 82. "Fleece Piece" first appeared in the Fall '00 issue of *Family Circle Easy Knitting* magazine.

## MATERIALS

- *Cleckheaton Country 8-ply* by Plymouth Yarn, 1¾oz/50g balls, each approx 105yd/96m (wool)
  2 balls in #0288 royal (A) OR #2178 red (C)
  1 ball in #2185 caramel (D)
- *Baby Bouclé* by Bernat®, 4oz/113g balls, each approx 204yd/185m (acrylic/polyester)
  1 ball in #1890 white (E)
- One pair size 6 (4mm) needles OR SIZE TO OBTAIN GAUGE
- Size F/5 (4mm) crochet hook
- 10"/25cm square pillow form
- Three ⅝"/15mm buttons
- Bobbins (optional)

## FINISHED MEASUREMENTS

- Approx 10"/25cm square

## GAUGE

20 sts and 26 rows to 4"/10cm over St st using size 6 (4mm) needles.
TAKE TIME TO CHECK YOUR GAUGE.

## Notes

**1** Pillow is worked in one piece.
**2** Use a separate ball of yarn for each block of color.
**3** When changing colors, twist yarns tog on WS to prevent holes.

## PILLOW

With A or C cast on 50 sts. Work in garter st for 12 rows. Beg with a p row, work in St st for 34 rows. K next row on WS for turning ridge. Work in St st for 12 rows.

## Beg chart

**Next row (RS)** K11, work 28 sts of chart, k11. Cont as established through row 36 of chart. Work 13 rows A or C. K next row on WS for turning ridge. Work in St st for 26 rows. Then work in garter st for 6 rows.

**Next (buttonhole) row** K11, *bind off 2 sts, k until there are 11 sts from bind-off; rep from * to end. K next row, casting on 2 sts over the bound-off sts. Cont in garter st for 4 rows more. Bind off.

## FINISHING

Block piece.

## LAMB

With A, work a French knot for eyes. With crochet hook and D, ch 8. Join with sl st to first ch. Sew center tog to close ear. See chart for placement. Fold pillow at turning ridges, WS tog, overlapping garter st bands and sew side seams. Sew buttons opposite buttonholes.

### Color Key

- ☐ Background color (MC)
- ✻ French knot with Blue (A)
- · Gold (C)
- ☒ White (B)
- ✐ Chain st with Gold (D)

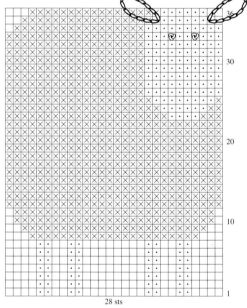

Set sail for dreamland with a whimsical baby blanket. The whale, fish and boat are knit in easy stockinette; embroidery, button and stockinette appliqués provide the details. "Whale's Tale" first appeared in the Spring/Summer '02 issue of *Family Circle Easy Knitting* magazine.

## MATERIALS

- *Super 10* by S.R. Kertzer Ltd., 4oz/125g skeins, each approx 249yd/230m (cotton)
  3 skeins in #3882 blue (A)
  1 skein each in 3423 red (B) and white (C), #3774 green (D), #3039 charcoal (E)
  and #3546 yellow (F)
- Size 6 (4mm) circular needle OR SIZE TO OBTAIN GAUGE
- Size E/4 (3.5mm) crochet hook
- One ³⁄₈"/10mm white button (eye)
- Small piece of red felt (for flag)
- Bobbins

## FINISHED MEASUREMENTS

- Approx 28" x 40"/71cm x 101.5cm

## GAUGE

20 sts and 24 rows to 4"/10cm over St st using larger needles.
TAKE TIME TO CHECK YOUR GAUGE.

## STRIPE PATTERN

*2 rows B, 2 rows C, rep frmo * (4 rows) for stripe pat.

## Note

Use a separate bobbin of yarn for each large block of color. When changing colors, twist yarns on WS to prevent holes in work.

With A, cast on 141 sts. Work in garter st for 8 rows.

**Next row (RS)** Cont 5 sts in garter st, work in St st to last 5 sts, cont 5 sts in garter st. Cont as established, keeping 5 sts each side in garter st with A throughout, for 4½"/11.5cm above garter st, end with a WS row.

## Beg charts

**Next row (RS)** Work 27 sts A, 20 sts chart 2, 47 sts A, 20 sts chart 1, 27 sts A. Cont as established until 19 rows of charts have been worked. Work 1 row with A on all sts.

**Next row (RS)** Work 55 sts A, 31 sts chart 3, 55 sts A. Cont as established until 43 rows of chart have been worked. Work 1 row with A on all sts.

**Next row (RS)** Work 27 sts A, 20 sts chart 1, 47 sts A, 20 sts chart 2, 27 sts A. Cont as established until 19 rows of charts have been worked. Work with A on all sts for 4"/10cm, end with a WS row.

## Beg chart 4

**Next row (RS)** K5 A (garter st border), work 3 sts B, [5 sts A, 3 sts B] 4 times, 2 sts A, work 50 sts chart 4, 1 st A, [3 sts B, 5 sts A] 5 times, 3 sts B, k5 A (garter st border). Cont as established, completing waves on either side of whale same as pullover (see chart 4), then cont these sts in stripe pat, until 45 rows of whale chart have been worked. Then cont all sts in stripe pat until there are 23 C stripes With A, work in garter st on all sts for 8 rows. Bind off.

## FINISHING

Block piece to measurements.

### Embellishments

For fish tail on green fish, with D, cast on 6 sts. Work in St st for 4 rows. Dec 1 st each side on next row, then every other row once more. Cut yarn and draw through rem 2 sts. Attach as indicated on chart 2.

For braided tail on red fish, with crochet hook, ch 1"/2.5cm and knot one end. make one each in B, D and F. Attach as indicated on chart 1.

For fish eyes, use French knots foll chart for placement and using D on chart 1 and B on chart 2.

For flag on boat, cut a piece of red felt foll chart 3 for pattern. Attach as indicated on one side.

For whale face, foll chart 5 and work chain st mouth with 3 strands B. Attach button for eye as indicated.

*(Charts on page 132 and 133)*

Barbara Venishnick's baby blanket transitions terrifically from playtime to naptime. Garter-stitched strips are sewn together, alternating directions of the squares. I-cord border and garter-stitch trim pull it all together. "Building Blocks" first appeared in the Winter '01/'02 issue of *Family Circle Easy Knitting* magazine.

## MATERIALS

- *Red Heart® Kids* by Coats & Clark™, 4oz/113g balls, each approx 242yd/223m (acrylic)
  2 balls each in #2652 lime (A) and #2845 blue (B)
  1 ball in #2940 blue/green (C)
- One pair size 7 (4.5mm) needles OR SIZE TO OBTAIN GAUGE
- Size 7 (4.5mm) circular needle, 40"/101.5cm long

## FINISHED MEASUREMENTS

- 28 x 24"/71 x 61cm

## GAUGE

18 sts and 36 rows to 4"/10cm over garter st using size 7 (4.5mm) needles.
TAKE TIME TO CHECK YOUR GAUGE

## Note

The blanket is made in long strips that are sewn together. The trim is picked up and worked around on the circular needle.

## STRIPS

(make 5 strips of six squares each)

### Square 1

With straight needles and A, cast on 18 sts.
**Rows 1-12** K1tbl, k16, sl 1 purlwise.
**Rows 13-24** With C, work as for rows 1-12.
Rows 25-36 With B, work as for rows 1-12. Leave all sts on needle and yarn still attached.

### Square 2

With straight needles and B, cast on 18 sts. Hold square 1 in left hand.
**Row 1** K1tbl, k16, k2tog (1 from square 1 and 1 from square 2).
**Row 2** K1tbl, k16, sl 1 purlwise.
**Rows 3-12** Rep rows 1 and 2.
**Rows 13-24** With C, rep rows 1-12. Rows 25-35

With A, rep rows 1-11. With WS facing and A, bind off 18 sts, leave last lp on needle, do not cut yarn.

### Square 3

Hold strip with WS facing. With A, pick up 17 sts purlwise along the side edge of square 2—18 sts. The last lp of square 2 counts as first st of square 3. Complete as for square 1.

### Square 4

Complete as for square 2.

### Square 5

Complete as for square 3.

### Square 6

Complete as for square 2. At the end of the final bind off, cut yarn and weave in end.

## FINISHING

### Assemble strips

Hold strip 1 with square 1 at the bottom and square 6 at the top. Place strip 2 next to it upside down, with square 6 at the bottom and square 1 at the top. Sew strips 1 and 2 tog in this position. Place strip 3 next to strip 2 RS up, with square 1 at bottom and square 6 at top. Sew strips 2 and 3 tog in this position. Cont in this way, alternating upside down and RS up strips until all 5 strips are sewn tog.

### Attached I-cord trim

With circular needle and C, cast on 4 sts. Hold blanket with RS facing and beg at any corner, with same needle and C, pick up 1 st in every cast-on or bound-off st, and every side selvege st. Work attached I-cord With RS facing, k3 of the cast on sts, k2tog (last cast on st and first picked up st). Sl 4 sts back to LH needle, DO NOT TURN. Bring yarn across back of work, k3, k2tog, sl 4 sts back to LH needle. Rep until the next corner is reached. At the corner, bring yarn across back of work and k4. Return to the attached method along the next side of the blanket. At each corner, work 1 row of unattached I-cord. When all picked up sts have been used, bind off 4 sts. Sew beg to end of I-cord.

### Garter st border

With circular needle and B, hold work with RS facing. Push I-cord down with thumb and pick up 1 st in each place where a color C st for I-cord was picked up. Place a marker at each corner. Join in a circle.
**Rnd 1** *K1, M1, work to 1 st before next marker, M1, k1; rep from * around.
**Rnd 2** Purl. Rep last 2 rnds 5 times more.
**Rnd 13** With A, work as for rnd 1.
**Rnd 14** With A, bind off purlwise.

A vintage-style throw in pretty pastels is the perfect portable project. Squares are knit individually, then sewn together to form a flower pattern at the center. Crochet edging completes the look. "Tickled Pink" first appeared in the Winter '01/'02 issue of *Family Circle Easy Knitting* magazine.

## MATERIALS

▪ *Merino Soft* by Schoeller Esslinger/Skacel, 1¾oz/50g balls, each approx 140yd/130m (wool)
  3 balls each in #42 dark lilac (A); #41 dark pink (B); #40 pink (C); #21 lilac (D)
▪ One pair size 5 (3.75mm) needles OR SIZE TO OBTAIN GAUGE
▪ Size E/4 (3.5mm) crochet hook

## FINISHED MEASUREMENTS

▪ 34 x 25"/86 x 63.5cm

## GAUGE

22 sts and 24 rows to 4"/10cm over garter st using size 5 (3.75mm) needles.
TAKE TIME TO CHECK YOUR GAUGE.

### Petal square

(Knit 12 squares of each color)
Beg at corner with raised petal, cast on 4 sts.
**Row 1 (RS)** Ktbl across. **Row 2** K2, yo, k2. **Row 3** and every RS row through row 17 Knit. **Row 4** K2, yo, k1, yo, k2. Row 6 K2, yo, k1, yo, p1, yo, k1, yo, k2.
**Row 8** K2, yo, k1, p2, yo, p1, yo, p2, k1, yo, k2—15 sts.
**Row 10** K2, yo, k2, p3, yo, p1, yo, p3, k2, yo, k2—19 sts.
**Row 12** K2, yo, k3, p4, yo, p1, yo, p4, k3, yo, k2—23 sts.
**Row 14** K2, yo, k4, p5, yo, p1, yo, p5, k4, yo, k2—27 sts.
**Row 16** K2, yo, k5, p6, yo, p1, yo, p6, k5, yo, k2—31 sts.
**Row 18** K2, yo, k6, p7, yo, p1, yo, p7, k6, yo, k2—35 sts.
**Row 19** K9, SKP, k13, k2tog, k9—33 sts.
**Row 20** K2, yo, k7, p15, k7, yo, k2—35 sts.
**Row 21** K10, SKP, k11, k2tog, k10—33 sts.

**Row 22** K2, yo, k8, p13, k8, yo, k2 —35 sts. Row 23 K11, SKP, k9, k2tog, k11—33 sts.
**Row 24** K2, yo, k9, p11, k9, yo, k2—35 sts.
**Row 25** K12, SKP, k7, k2tog, k12—33sts.
**Row 26** K2, yo, k10, p9, k10, yo, k2—35 sts.
**Row 27** K13, SKP, k5, k2tog, k13—33 sts.
**Row 28** K2, yo, k11, p7, k11, yo, k2—35 sts
**Row 29** K14, SKP, k3, k2tog, k14—33 sts.
**Row 30** K2, yo, k12, p5, k12, yo, k2—35 sts.
**Row 31** K15, SKP, k1, k2tog, k15—33 sts.
**Row 32** K2, yo, k13, p3, k13, yo, k2—35 sts.
**Row 33** K16, SK2P, k16—33 sts.
**Row 34** K2, yo, k29, yo, k2—35 sts. This completes ½ of square. Dec as foll:
**Row 35** K3, k2tog, k25, k2tog, k3—33 sts. **Row 36** K2, yo, k2tog, k25, k2tog, yo, k2. **Row 37** K3, k2tog, k23, k2tog, k3—31 sts. **Row 38** K2, yo, k2tog, k23, k2tog, yo, k2. **Row 39** K3, k2tog, k21, k2tog, k3—29 sts. **Row 40** K2, yo, k2tog, k21, k2tog, yo, k2. **Row 41** K3, k2tog, k19, k2tog, k3—27 sts. **Row 42** K2, yo, k2tog, k19, k2tog, yo, k2. **Row 43** K3, k2tog, k17, k2tog, k3—25 sts. **Row 44** K2, yo, k2tog, k17, k2tog, yo, k2. **Row 45** K3, k2tog, k15, k2tog, k3—23 sts. **Row 46** K2, yo, k2tog, k15, k2tog, yo, k2. **Row 47** K3, k2tog, k13, k2tog, k3—21 sts. **Row 48** K2, yo, k2tog, k13, k2tog, yo, k2. **Row 49** K3, k2tog, k11, k2tog, k3—19 sts. **Row 50** K2, yo, k2tog, k11, k2tog, yo, k2.

**Row 51** K3, k2tog, k9, k2tog, k3—17 sts. **Row 52** K2, yo, k2tog, k9, k2tog, yo, k2. **Row 53** K3, k2tog, k7, k2tog, k3—15 sts.
**Row 54** K2, yo, k2tog, k7, k2tog, yo, k2.
**Row 55** K3, k2tog, k5, k2tog, k3—13 sts.
**Row 56** K2, yo, k2tog, k5, k2tog, yo, k2.
**Row 57** K3, k2tog, k3, k2tog, k3—11 sts.
**Row 58** K2, yo, k2tog, k3, k2tog, yo, k2.
**Row 59** K3, k2tog, k1, k2tog, k3—9 sts.
**Row 60** K2, yo, k2tog, k1, k2tog, yo, k2.
**Row 61** K3, k2tog, k1, k3.
**Row 62** K2, yo, k2tog twice, yo, k2.
**Row 63** K3, k2tog, k3.
**Row 64** K2tog 3 times, k1.
Bind off.

## FINISHING

Foll diagram, sew squares tog.

### Crochet edging

**Rnd 1** With RS of blanket facing, attach D to side edging. Ch 1, sc in same space, sc in every st to corner, 3 sc in corner, sc to first sc. With C, sl st into first sc.

**Rnd 2** Sc in back loop of first sc, *long sc in sc of first row (by working into base of sc, not top lp), sc in back loop of next sc, rep from * to corner, at corner, work long sc, ch2, long sc; cont in this way around.

*(Diagram on page 132)*

Stitch up this jewel-toned treasure for your little gem. Margarita Mejia's colorful design is composed of multi-hued granny squares that are crocheted separately, then sewn together with main color. Delicate picot edging provides the perfect finishing touch. "Bright Idea" first appeared in the Winter '01/'02 issue of *Family Circle Easy Knitting* magazine.

## MATERIALS

- *Baby-Ull* by Garnstudio/Aurora Yarns, 1¾oz/50g balls, each approx 189yd/175m (wool)
  3 balls in #21 red (MC)
  1 ball each in #06 pink (A), #07 coral (B), #24 orange (C) and #09 purple (D)
- Size E/4 (3.5mm) crochet hook OR SIZE TO OBTAIN GAUGE

## FINISHED MEASUREMENTS

- Approx 20"/50.5cm x 26"/66cm

## GAUGE

One square to 3¼"/8.5cm using size E/4 (3.5mm) crochet hook.
TAKE TIME TO CHECK YOUR GAUGE.

## BASIC GRANNY SQUARE

With first color, ch 5. Join with sl st to first ch to form ring.

**Rnd 1** Ch 3, work 2 dc in ring, [ch 3, work 3 dc in ring] 3 times, ch 3, join with sl st to top of ch-3 at beg of rnd. Fasten off.

**Rnd 2** Join 2nd color in any space made by ch-3. Ch 3, 1 dc in same space, [dc in each of next 3 dc, in next ch-3 sp work 2 dc, ch 3 and 2 dc] 3 times, dc in each of next 3 dc, 2 dc in same sp at beg of rnd. Fasten off.

**Rnd 3** Join 3rd color in any space made by ch-3. Ch 3, 1 dc in same space, [dc in each of next 7 dc, in next ch-3 sp work 2 dc, ch 3 and 2 dc] 3 times, dc in each of next 7 dc, 2 dc in same sp at beg of rnd. Fasten off.

**Rnd 4** With MC, rep rnd 3, working 11 dc between corners.

Make squares follow placement diagram for colorways.

## FINISHING

With MC, crochet squares tog foll placement diagram.

### Edging

With RS facing and MC, work as foll: join MC to any corner ch-3 space, work 3 dc in same space, *ch 3, sl st in 3nd ch, sk 3 dc, work 3 dc in next dc; rep from * to next corner, work 6 dc in corner ch-3 sp, cont in this way around entire blanket. Join and fasten off.

### Placement Diagram

| | | | | | |
|---|---|---|---|---|---|
| B, D, A | A, B, C | MC, C, D | C, D, A | D, C, B | A, C, D |
| D, B, C | B, A, D | D, B, A | MC, A, C | C, B, D | B, D, C |
| C, A, D | C, A, B | B, C, D | A, C, B | MC, D, A | C, A, D |
| A, D, B | MC, C, D | D, A, C | D, B, A | A, C, D | D, B, A |
| D, B, A | D, C, B | B, A, D | MC, B, C | C, D, A | A, D, B |
| C, A, D | MC, D, A | C, A, B | B, C, D | D, A, C | C, A, D |
| B, D, C | C, B, D | MC, A, C | D, B, A | B, A, D | D, B, C |
| A, C, D | D, C, B | C, D, A | MC, C, D | A, B, C | B, D, A |

**Color Key**
Pink (A)
Coral (B)
Orange (C)
Purple (D)

# Barn Dance

Friendly farm animals border Amy Bahrt's bold striped blanket. The fanciful sheep, duck and pig motifs can be knit in one piece or stitched separately and sewn around the striped center. "Barn Dance" first appeared in the Winter '01/'02 issue of *Family Circle Easy Knitting* magazine.

## MATERIALS

▪ *Provence* by Classic Elite Yarns, 4oz/125g balls, each approx 256yd/236m (cotton)

 3 balls in #2648 blue (A)

 2 balls each in #2625 pink (B) and #2681 green (D)

 1 ball each in #2633 yellow (C); #2613 black (E) and #2601 white (F)

▪ Size 6 (4mm) circular needle, 40"/101.5cm long OR SIZE TO OBTAIN GAUGE

## FINISHED MEASUREMENTS

▪ 32 x 36"/81 x 91.5cm

## GAUGE

20 sts and 24 rows to 4"/10cm over St st using size 6 (4mm) needle.
TAKE TIME TO CHECK YOUR GAUGE.

## Notes

**1** Border: For the entire length of blanket, the first and last 5 sts are worked with D in garter st. The body of the blanket is worked in St st.
**2** Each square is 28 sts and 34 rows.
**3** The number on the placement diagram within the animal represents the chart # to be knit in that position.
**4** The squares may be knit separately, if desired, and sewn together using the placement diagram.
**5** To avoid holes, twist yarns when changing colors

## STRIPE PATTERN

*In St st, work 4 rows B, 4 row D; rep from *.

## BLANKET

With D, cast on 158 sts. Work in garter st for 8 rows. **Next row (RS)** Work border as described in note 1, *k28 sts A (square), 2 sts D (inside border); rep from * 3 times more, end with 28 st A work border—5 squares, with 4 inside borders have been established. Cont as established for 5 rows.

### Beg charts

Cont working squares and inside borders as established, AT SAME TIME, work charts as noted on diagram, centered within each square. Work through 34 rows.
**Next row (RS)** Work 2 rows D (sts 6-34 and sts 124-152 form side borders).
**Next row (RS)** Work border, k28 sts A (side square), 92 sts D, 28 sts A (side square), work border. Work even for 1 row.
**Next row (RS)** Work border, k28 sts A, beg stripe pat over next 92 sts, work 28 sts A, work border. Cont as established for 7 rows.

### Beg charts

Cont in pats as established, AT SAME TIME, work charts as noted on diagram, centered within each square. Cont working until all side squares are completed and stripe pat ends with 4 rows B. Work 2 rows D.
**Next row (RS)** Establish squares and inside borders as for bottom squares, using diagram for placement of charts. Work through row 34 rows. With D work 8 rows garter st. Bind off.

## FINISHING

Block lightly.

### LAMB

**Ears**

With E, form 8-st chain lp, sew the center of lp tog and tack down. Foll chart and photo for placement.

**Eyes**

With A, work french knot, foll chart and photo for placement.

### PIG

Ears With B, form 7-st chain lp, sew the center of lp tog and tack down. Foll chart and photo for placement.

**Eyes**

With A, work french knot, foll chart and photo for placement.

**Tail**

With B, form 12-st chain lp, and tack down in a swirl. Foll chart and photo for placement.

**Nose**

With B, form 10-st chain loop, sew the center of loop tog and tack down. Foll chart and photo for placement.

### DUCK

**Wing**

With C, cast on 7 sts. Work in St st for 4 rows, then dec 1 st each side every other row until 1 st rem. Pull strand through lp and tack down. Foll chart and photo for placement.

**Eyes**

With D, work french knot, foll chart and photo for placement.

*(Charts on page 134)*

# Toy Box

Soft-sculpture pals make playtime fun.

# Rainbow Teddy

## for advanced knitters

So bear-y cute, this colorful cuddler will be adored by children of all ages. He's knit in simple sections of stockinette, then embroidered with a medley of decorative stitches including lazy daisy, blanket, feather and straight stitch. "Rainbow Teddy" first appeared in the Fall '96 issue of *Family Circle Knitting* magazine.

## MATERIALS

- *Caprice* by Plymouth Yarns, 1¾oz/50g, approx 145yd/132m (acrylic)
  1 ball each of #1583 royal blue (A), #1517 orange (B), #1611 green (C), #1641 purple (D), #1628 dk pink (E), #1632 lime (F), #1516 yellow (G), #1511 turquoise (H), #1506 red (I)

The above colors make a very bright and cheerful teddy, for a more mellow teddy, the knitter can also use *Country 8 Ply* by Cleckheaton/ Plymouth Yarns in softer colors.

- One pair size 8 (5mm) needles
- Small amount of black yarn for embroidery
- 1 pair size 5 (3.75mm) needles OR SIZE TO OBTAIN GAUGE
- Stitch holder
- Polyester fiberfill stuffing
- Yarn needle

## FINISHED MEASUREMENTS

- Size approx 14"/35.5cm tall

## GAUGE

24 sts and 34 rows to 4"/10cm in St st using size 8 (5mm) needles.
TAKE TIME TO CHECK YOUR GAUGE.

## STITCH GLOSSARY

### 2-st Dec Row

Work across to 2 sts before marker, dec, slip marker, dec, work across.

### 4-st Dec Row

Dec at beg of row, work across to 2 sts before marker, dec, slip marker, dec, work across to last 2 sts, dec.

### 2-st Inc Row

Work across and inc in st right before an right after marker.

### 4-st Inc Row

Inc at beg of row, work across and inc in st right before and right after marker, work across and inc in last st.

### Notes

Bear is worked in St st.

**1** Color is worked using the Intarsia method: use a separate skein of yarn for each color area.
**2** When changing colors in middle of row at marker, drop old color to WS and pick up new color from underneath. This will twist both yarns tog to avoid a hole.
**3** Decorate finished teddy with embroidery stitches.

## BACK

Cast on 2 sts with B, place marker (PM), then cast on 2 sts with A—4 sts. Working in colors as established, inc in each st across—8 sts. Work 2-st Inc Row on next row—10 sts. Work 4-st Inc Row on next row—14 sts. Work 2-st Inc Row on next 3 rows—20 sts. Work 4-st Inc Row on next row—24 sts. P next row.
**Next Row** *Work 2-st Inc Row, p next row—26 sts. Work 4-st Inc Row, p next row—30 sts. Rep from * until there are 42 sts, end with WS row. Work 2 rows even.
**Next Row** Work 4-st Inc Row—46 sts.
**Next Row (WS)** Work in St st, inc 1 st at each end of every 4th row twice—50 sts. Then work 5 rows even in St st. Change colors

**Next Row (RS)** K25 with C, k 25 with D. Working in colors as established, dec 1 st each end of every 4th row 4 times, end with a RS row—42 sts.
**Next Row (WS)** Work 2-st Dec Row on next 3 rows—36 sts. Work 4-st Dec Row on next row—32 sts. Work 2-st Dec Row on next 3 rows—26 sts. Work 4-st Dec Row on next 2 rows. Bind off rem 18 sts.

## FRONT

Cast on as for Back. K2 with A, k2 with B. Working in colors as established. P 1 row, then inc in each st across on next row—8 sts.
**Next Row** *Work 2-st Inc Row, p next row. Work 4-st Inc Row, p next row. Rep from * until there are 50 sts. Work 2 rows even, inc 1 st each end of next row, work 1 row even. Change colors
**Next Row (RS)** K26 with C, k26 with D. Working in colors as established, work 5 rows even in St st.
**Next Row** [Work 4-st Dec Row, then work 3 rows even] 3 times—40 sts.
**Next Row (RS)** [Work 4-st Dec Row, p next row.

*(Continued on page 135)*

# Funny Bunny

for advanced knitters

This floppy-eared friend is worked in simple stitches using two strands of yarn held together for super-quick knitting. Dressed in dapper shortalls trimmed with whip-stitched stripes, "Funny Bunny" first appeared in the Fall '99 issue of *Family Circle Easy Knitting* magazine.

## MATERIALS

*Bunny*

- ▨ *Bebé Lang* by Lang/Berroco, Inc., 1¾oz/50g balls, each approx 219yd/203m (wool)
  1 ball each in #7102 ecru (A) and #7120 lt blue (B)
- ▨ One pair size 8 (5mm) needles OR SIZE TO OBTAIN GAUGE
- ▨ Small amount of black yarn for eyes and nose
- ▨ Stitch holders and fiberfill

*Shortalls*

- ▨ *Omega* by Lang/Berroco, Inc., 1¾oz/50g balls, each approx 108yd/100m (cotton)
  1 ball each in #2932 blue (MC) and #2903 white (CC)
- ▨ One pair size 6 (4mm) needles OR SIZE TO OBTAIN GAUGE
- ▨ Two buttons

## FINISHED MEASUREMENTS
- ▨ 14"/35.6cm tall

## GAUGES

*Bunny*

- ▨ 20 sts and 28 rows to 4"/10cm over St st using size 8 (5mm) needles and 1 strand each A and B held tog.

*Shortalls*

- ▨ 21 sts and 26 rows to 4"/10cm over St st using size 6 (4mm) needles.

TAKE TIME TO CHECK YOUR GAUGES.

## BUNNY

**Note**

Work with 1 strand each of A and B held tog throughout.

### HEAD

**Side**

Cast on 13 sts. K 2 rows.

**Row 3 (WS)** Purl. Cont in St st as foll: **Row 4** Inc 1 st in first st, k to end. Work 3 rows even. Rep last 4 rows twice more—16 sts.

**Row 16 (RS)** Bind off 3 sts, k to end. Work 1 row even. **Row 18** Bind off 2 sts, k to last 2 sts, dec 1 st. Work 1 row even. Rep last 2 rows once more. **Row 22** Bind off 2 sts, k to end. Work 1 row even. Bind off rem 5 sts. Work 2nd side to correspond, reversing shaping.

**Center**

Cast on 10 sts. K 2 rows. Beg with a p row, cont in St st for 25 rows. **Row 28** Dec 1 st each side. Work 5 rows even. Rep last 6 rows twice more. Bind off rem 4 sts.

Sew sides of head to center of head and stuff. Embroider eyes and nose foll photo.

**Ears** (make 2)

Cast on 16 sts. Work in garter st for 13 rows. Dec 1 st each side on next row. Work 5 rows even. Dec 1 st each side on next row. Work 3 rows even. Rep last 10 rows twice more. Bind off rem 4 sts. Sew to top of head foll photo for placement.

**Arms** (make 2)

Cast on 6 sts and work in St st, inc 1 st each side every other row 7 times—20 sts. Work even until there are 30 rows from beg. Dec 1 st each side on next row, then every 3rd row 3 times more. Bind off rem 12 sts. Sew seams and stuff.

### BACK

**BODY**

Cast on 28 sts. Beg with a p row and work in St st for 19 rows.

**Next row (RS)** Work 14 sts, join 2nd ball of yarn and work to end. Cont to work both sides at once with separate balls of yarn, work 1 row even.

**Dec row 1 (RS)** Dec 1 st, work to end of first half; on 2nd half, work to last 2 sts, dec 1 st. Work 3 rows even. [Dec row 2 Dec 1 st, work to last 2 sts of first side, dec 1 st; on 2nd side dec 1 st each side. Work 3 rows even] 3 times. Bind off rem 7 sts each side.

### LEGS

Cast on 13 sts and work in St st for 42 rows. Place sts on a holder. Work a 2nd leg in same way. Join both legs and work even on 26 sts for 2 rows. Dec 1 st each side on next row. Work 3 rows even. [Dec 1 st each side of next row. Work 1 row even] 5 times. Work 4 rows even. Bind off rem 14 sts. Sew cast-on edge of back to bound-off edge of legs, foll diagram. Sew center seam of back.

### BODY FRONT

Cast on 13 sts for one leg and work in St st for 42 rows. Place sts on a holder. Work a 2nd leg in same way. Join both legs and work even all 26 sts for 20 rows.

**Next row (RS)** Work 13 sts, join 2nd ball of yarn

*(Continued on page 136)*

# Elephant March
## for intermediate knitters

Small hands are guaranteed to grab for these captivating pachyderms designed by Jacqueline Van Dillen. Easy to knit from her floppy ears to her chain-stitch tail, she's the perfect partner for your bundle of joy. "Elephant March" first appeared in the Spring/Summer '01 issue of *Family Circle Easy Knitting* magazine.

## MATERIALS

- *Windsurf* by Sesia/Colorado Yarns, 1¾oz/50g balls, each approx 150yd/108m (cotton) 2 balls in #203 blue or #68 pink
- One pair size 3 (3mm) needles OR SIZE TO OBTAIN GAUGE
- Small piece of felt for eyes
- ¾yd/.75m of grosgrain ribbon ⅝"/15mm wide
- Fiberfill for stuffing

## GAUGE

26 sts and 40 rows to 2½"/6cm over garter st using size 3 (3mm) needles.
TAKE TIME TO CHECK YOUR GAUGE.

**Inc 1**
**At beg of row** K1, k in front and back of st—1 st inc'd.
**At end of row** Work to last 2 sts, k in front and back of next st, k1.

**Inc 2**
**At beg of row** K1, inc 1 st in each of next 2 sts.
**At end of row** Work to last 3 sts, inc 1 st in each of next 2 sts, k1.

## BODY

(make 2)
Cast on 24 sts for center bottom. Work in garter st, inc at RH side as foll: 2 sts 7 times, 1 st 8 times, AT SAME TIME, inc at LH side as foll: 2 sts 7 times, 1 st 10 times—70 sts. Work even until there are 40 rows from beg.

**Neck shaping**
**Next row** Bind off 16 sts (neck edge), work to end and place a marker. Cont to dec 1 st at neck edge every other row 7 times, every 4th row 4 times, AT SAME TIME, on other side work 16 rows even above marker, then dec 1 st on next row, then every 4th row twice, every other row 3 times, then dec 2 sts (k3tog) every other row 7 times. Bind off rem 23 sts.

## TRUNK AND HEAD

Beg with trunk, cast on 11 sts. Work in garter st as foll: Work even for 6 rows. Inc 2 sts each side on next row, then every 4th row twice more, AT SAME TIME, dec 2 sts at center (k 3 center sts tog) on next row, then every 4th row 3 times more—15 sts. Work 6 rows even. Mark center st. Inc 1 st each side of center st on next row, then every 8th row once, every 6th row once, every 10th row once, AT SAME TIME, after 32 rows have been worked from beg, inc 1 st each side of row, then work 7 rows even and inc 1 st each side of next row, then every other row once, inc 2 sts each side every other row 6 times, inc 1 st each side every other row twice, every 4th row twice—61 sts. Work 3 rows even, then dec 2 sts at center as before on next row, then every 4th row 7 times more, AT SAME TIME, after 76 rows have been worked from beg, dec 1 st each side of next row, then every 4th row 3 times more, every other row 4 times—29 sts. Bind off.

## LEGS

(make 4)
Cast on 4 sts. Work in garter st as foll: Inc 2 sts each side every other row 5 times, inc 1 st each side every other row once—26 sts. Work even for 20 rows.
**Next row** *K2tog; rep from* to end—13 sts.
**Next row** K1, *k2tog; rep from * to end. Bind off rem 7 sts.

## EARS

(make 2)
Cast on 5 sts. Work in garter st as foll: Work 2 rows even. Next row Inc 1 st in each st—10 sts. On RH side, inc 2 sts every other row 3 times, AT SAME TIME, on LH side, inc 2 sts every other row once, 1 st every other row once, every 4th row once—20 sts. Work even until there are 32 rows from beg. On LH side, dec 1 st on next row, then every 4th row 3 times, every other row once, then dec 2 sts every 4th row once, AT SAME TIME, on RH side, work 6 rows even, then dec 1 st on next row, then every 4th row once, then every other row twice, dec 2 sts every other row once. Bind off rem 7 sts.

## TAIL

Cast on 13 sts. Work in garter st as foll: Work 6 rows even, then dec 1 st each side on next row, then every other row 4 times more—3 sts. Work even until there are 40 rows from beg. Bind off.

## FINISHING

Sew two pieces of body tog along bottom and top edge. Stuff. Sew side of each leg, stuff and sew to lower edge of body. Attach head to neck of body, leaving an opening, stuff and sew opening closed. Attach ears and tail. Cut two small felt circles and sew on for eyes.

# Toby Triceratop
## for intermediate knitters

Kids go crazy for dinosaurs! Sporting his own sweater and plenty of attitude, he'll be a treasured friend for your budding paleontologist. "Toby Triceratop" first appeared in the Winter '97/'98 issue of *Family Circle Knitting* magazine.

## MATERIALS

- *Astra* by Patons® 1¾oz/50g skein, each approx 178yd/163m (acrylic)
  - 2 skeins in #2763 blue (MC)
  - 1 skein each of #2874 yellow (A), #2751 white (B) and #2746 green (C)
  - Small amount of #2765 black (D)
- 1 pair size 5 (3.75 mm) needles OR SIZE TO OBTAIN GAUGE
- Stitch holder
- Polyester fiberfill
- Green felt
- Craft glue

## FINISHED MEASUREMENTS

- 20"/51cm tall

## GAUGE

23 sts and 31 rows to 4"/10cm over St st, using size 5 (3.75 mm) needles.
TAKE TIME TO CHECK YOUR GAUGE.

### Notes

**1** When changing colors in the middle of a row, twist the color to be used (on WS) underneath and to the right of the color just used.
**2** Use separate ball of yarn for each color.
**3** When binding off, the last st on RH needle is the first st of the stitch count that directly follows.

## LEFT LEG

### Sole

** With size 5 (3.75 mm) needles and MC, cast on 5 sts.

**Row 1 (RS)** Knit. Work in garter st, inc 1 st each side of every row 3 times, then every other row 3 times—17 sts. Work even until piece measures 4"/10cm from beg, end with a WS row. Change to B, work in St st, AT SAME TIME, dec 1 st each side on 3rd row, then every other row 3 times, then every row once. Bind off rem 7 sts.

### Top of foot

Cast on 80 sts as foll: 26 sts MC, 28 sts B, 26 sts MC. K 1 row and p 1 row matching colors.

### Shape toes

**Row 3** K26 MC, *k8 B, k2 MC; rep from * twice more, k24 MC.
**Row 4** P26 MC, *(p2tog, p4, p2tog tbl) B, p2 MC; rep from * twice more, p24 MC—74 sts.
**Row 5** (K25, M1, k1) MC, *k6 B, (k1, M1, k1) MC; rep from * twice more, k24 MC—78 sts.
**Row 6** P27 MC, *(p2tog, p2, p2tog tbl) B, p3 MC; rep from * twice more, p24 MC—72 sts.
**Row 7** [K25, M1, k1] twice MC, (SKP, k2tog) B, (k1, M1, k2) MC, (SKP, k2tog) B, (k2, M1, k1) MC, (SKP, k2tog) B, [(k1, M1) twice, k25] MC—72 sts. Break B. With MC, work 5 rows St st.

### Shape ankle

**Next row (RS)** K21, [k3tog] 10 times, k21—52 sts.** Work 16 rows even.
**Next row** Bind off 26 sts, p to end—26 sts.

### Shape thigh and tail opening

**Row 1 (RS)** Bind off 3 sts, k2, [M1, k6] 3 times, k3—26 sts.
**Row 2 and all WS** rows Purl.
**Row 3** Bind off 2 sts, k8, M1, k7, M1, k6, M1, k3—27 sts.
**Row 5** Bind off 2 sts, k7, M1, k8, M1, k7, M1, k3—28 sts.
**Row 7** Bind off 2 sts, k6, M1, k9, M1, k11—28 sts. Work 7 rows even. Work 3 more rows St st, AT SAME TIME, cast on 2 sts at beg of each RS row—32 sts.
**Next row (WS)** Bind off 6 sts, p to end—26 sts.

**Next row** Cast on 2 sts, k to end—28 sts.
**Next row** Bind off 6 sts, p to end—22 sts.
**Next row** Cast on 3 sts, k to end—25 sts. Cont in St st, bind off 6 sts at beg of every WS row 3 times. Work 1 row even. Bind off rem 7 sts.

## RIGHT LEG

Work as for left leg from ** to **. Work 17 rows even.

### Shape thigh and tail opening

**Row 1** Bind off 26 sts, k9, (M1, K6) twice, M1, k5—29 sts.
**Row 2** Bind off 3 sts, p to end—26 sts.
**Row 3** K3, M1, k6, M1, k7, M1, k10—29 sts.
**Row 4** Bind off 2 sts, p to end—27 sts.
**Row 5** K3, M1, k7, M1, k8, M1, k9—30 sts.
**Row 6** Rep row 4—28 sts.
**Row 7** K11, M1, k9, M1, k8—30 sts.
**Row 8** Rep row 4—28 sts. Work 5 rows even. Work 3 more rows St st, AT SAME TIME, cast on 2 sts at beg of every WS row twice—32 sts.
**Next row (RS)** Bind off 6 sts, k to end—26 sts.
**Next row** Cast on 2 sts, p to end—28 sts.
**Next row** Bind off 6 sts, k to end—22 sts.
**Next row** Cast on 3 sts, p to end—25 sts. Cont in St st, bind off 6 sts at beg of every RS row 3 times. Work 1 row even. Bind off rem 7 sts.

## TAIL AND GUSSET

With MC, cast on 12 sts. Work 6 rows St st.

*(Continued on page 136)*

# Barnyard Buddies

A pink pig and a cool cat will amuse country and city kids alike. Gitta Schrade interpreted these cuddly designs, stitching them in machine-washable acrylic for easy-care. "Barnyard Buddies" first appeared in the Spring/Summer '98 issue of *Family Circle Easy Knitting* magazine.

## MATERIALS

▪ *Astra* by Patons®, 1³/₄oz/50g skeins, each approx 178yd/163m (acrylic)

*Cat*

   1 skein in #2774 lt blue (A)

   Small amounts in #2765 black (B) and #2912 med green (C) for embroidery

*Pig*

   1 skein in #2210 med pink (A)

   Small amounts in #2895 dk pink (B) and #2765 black (C)

▪ Size C/2 (2.5mm) crochet hook

*For both*

▪ One pair size 2 (2.5mm) needles OR SIZE TO OBTAIN GAUGE

▪ Stitch holder

▪ Polyester fiberfill

▪ Tapestry needle

## GAUGE

27 sts and 36 rows to 4"/10cm over St st (unstuffed) using size 2 (2.5mm) needles. TAKE TIME TO CHECK YOUR GAUGE.

### Note

Work cat foll chart in St st for first side, and in reverse St st for 2nd side. Work incs or decs either side of row foll chart. When 2 or more boxes are used in shaping, cast on or bind off sts joining a new ball of yarn when necessary.

## CAT

### First side

With A, cast on 7 sts for back leg. Work in St st foll chart through row 26. Place sts on a holder. Cast on 7 sts for front leg. Work in St st foll chart through row 26.

**Row 27 (RS)** Work 18 sts of front leg, cast on 5 sts, work 16 sts of back leg—39 sts. Cont to foll chart as before until chart is completed (row 69). Bind off rem 5 sts.

### Second side

Working in reverse St st, work as for first side.

### Band

With A, cast on 9 sts. Work in St st for approx 45"/114cm and place sts on a holder for adjustment.

### FINISHING

Do not block pieces. Sew band all around outlines of cat, joining both sides. Leave opening at center for stuffing. Bind off sts to fit after adjusting. Stuff head with fiberfill. Using chart and photo as a guide, embroider face. Finish stuffing and sew final seam.

## PIG

### Note

Work cat foll chart in St st for first side, and in reverse St st for 2nd side. Work incs or decs either side of row foll chart. When 2 or more boxes are used in shaping, cast on or bind off sts joining a new ball of yarn when necessary.

### First side

With A, cast on 7 sts for front leg. Work in St st foll chart through row 16. Place sts on a holder. Cast on 8 sts for tummy section and work 4 rows foll chart. Place sts on a holder. Cast on 8 sts for back leg. Work in St st foll chart through row 16.

**Row 17 (RS)** Working across back leg, inc 1 st, work to last st, inc 1 st in last st, inc 1 st in first st of tummy sts, work to last st, inc 1 st in last st, work rem sts of front leg. Cont to foll chart as before until chart is completed (row 50). Bind off.

### Second side

Working in reverse St st, work as for first side.

### Band

With A, cast on 9 sts. Work in St st for approx 34"/86cm and place sts on a holder for adjustment.

### FINISHING

Do not block pieces. Sew band all around outlines of pig, joining both sides. Leave opening at center for stuffing. Bind off sts to fit after adjusting. Stuff head with fiberfill.

### Nose

With crochet hook and B, ch 3. Join with sl st to first ch to form ring.

**Rnd 1** Work 6 sc in ring. Join, ch 1.

**Rnd 2** Work 2 sc in each sc around—12 sc. Join, ch 1.

*(Continued on page 138)*

# Betsy Brachiosaurus

## for intermediate knitters

A delightful dinosaur makes a super Jurassic playpen friend. With her fringed eyelashes and bright spots, she's sure to light up any room. "Betsy Brachiosaurus" first appeared in the Winter '97/'98 issue off *Family Circle Knitting* magazine.

## MATERIALS

- *Astra* by Patons® 1³⁄₄oz/50g skein, each approx 178yd/163m (acrylic)
  1 skein in pink #2211 (MC),
  1 skein each of #2874 yellow (A) and #2751 white (B)
- Small amount of #2765 black (C)
- 1 pair size 5 (3.75mm) needles OR SIZE TO OBTAIN GAUGE
- Polyester fiberfill
- Blue felt
- Craft glue

## FINISHED MEASUREMENTS

18"/46cm tall.

## GAUGE

23 sts and 31 rows to 4"/10cm over St st, using size 5 (3.75mm) needles.
TAKE TIME TO CHECK YOUR GAUGE.

## STITCH GLOSSARY

### SK2P

Sl 1, k2tog, pass sl st over.

## Note

**1** When changing colors in the middle of a row, twist the color to be used (on WS) underneath and to the right of the color just used.
**2** Use a separate ball of yarn for each section of color.
**3** When binding off, the last st on RH needle is the first st of the stitch count that directly follows.

## LEFT LEG

### Sole

**With size 5 (3.75mm) needles and A, cast on 7 sts. **Row 1 (RS)** Knit. Work in garter st, inc 1 st each side of every row 4 times, then every other row twice—19 sts. Work even until piece measures 4¹⁄₄"/11cm from beg, end with a RS row. **Next row (WS)** With B, work in St st, dec 1 st each side of 4th row, then every other row twice more, then every row 3 times. Bind off rem 7 sts.

### Top of foot

Cast on 92 sts as foll: 32 sts MC, 28 sts B, 32 sts MC. K 1 row, p 1 row, matching colors.**

### Shape toes

**Row 3** K32 MC, *(SKP, k4, k2tog) B, k2 MC; rep from * once, k8 B, k32 MC—88sts. **Row 4** P32 MC, (p2tog, p4, p2tog tbl) B, *p2 MC, (p2tog, p2, p2tog tbl) B; rep from * once, p32 MC—82 sts. **Row 5** (K31, M1, k1) MC, *(SKP, k2tog) B, (k1, M1, k1) MC; rep from * once, k6 B, (k1, M1, k31) MC—82 sts. **Row 6** P33 MC, (p2tog, p2, p2tog tbl) B, p43 MC—80 sts. **Row 7** K43 MC, (SKP, k2tog) B, k33 MC—78 sts. ***With MC, work 5 rows St st, beg with a purl row.

### Shape ankle

**Next row** K24, (k3tog) 10 times, k24—58 sts. Work 9 rows even. **Next row** K26, (M1, k2) 3 times, M1, k26—62 sts. **Next row** Purl. Next row K25, M1, k3, M1, k6, M1, k3, M1, k25—66 sts.*** Work 6 rows even. **Next row (WS)** Bind off 33 sts, p to end—33 sts.

### Shape thigh and tail opening

**Row 1** Bind off 4 sts, k7, [M1, k7] 3 times, k1—32 sts. **Row 2** and all WS rows Purl. **Row 3** Bind off 4 sts, [M1, k8] 3 times, k3—31 sts. **Row 5** Bind off 2 sts, k2, [M1, k9] 3 times—32 sts. **Row 7** Bind off 2 sts, k6, [M1, k10] twice, k4. **Row 9** Bind off 2 sts, k2, [M1, k7] twice, k14. **Row 10** Purl. Work 9 rows

even. Bind off 4 sts at beg of next and every WS row 3 times—20 sts. **Next row (RS)** Cast on 2 sts, k to end—22 sts. **Next row** Bind off 4 sts, p to end—18 sts. **Next row** Cast on 4 sts, k to end—22 sts. Rep last 2 rows once, then first of these 2 rows once. **Next row** Knit. Bind off 4 sts at beg of next and every WS row 3 times. Work 1 row even. Bind off rem 6 sts.

## RIGHT LEG

Work as for left leg from ** to **.

### Shape toes

**Row 3** K32 MC, k8 B, *k2 MC, (SKP, K4, k2tog) B; rep from * once more, k32 MC—88 sts. **Row 4** P32 MC, *(p2tog, p2, p2tog tbl) B, p2 MC; rep from * once more, (p2tog, p4, p2tog tbl) B, p32 MC—82 sts. **Row 5** (K31, M1, k1) MC, k6 B, (k1, M1, k1) MC, *(SKP, k2tog) B, (k1, M1, k1) MC; rep from * once, k30 MC—82 sts. **Row 6** P43 MC, (p2tog, p2, p2tog tbl) B, p33 MC—80 sts. **Row 7** K33 MC, (SKP, K2tog) B, k43 MC—78 sts. Work as for left leg from *** to ***. Work 7 rows even.

### Shape thigh and tail opening

**Row 1** Bind off 33 sts, k8, (M1, k7) 3 times, k4—36 sts. **Row 2** Bind off 4 sts, p to end. **Row 3** K12, (M1, k8) twice, M1, k4—35 sts. **Row 4** Rep Row 2. **Row 5** (K9, M1) 3 times, k4—34 sts. **Row 6** Bind off 2 sts, p to end. **Row 7** K14, M1, k10, M1, k8—34 sts. **Row 8** Rep row 6. **Row 9** K21, M1, k7, M1, k4—34 sts. **Row 10** Bind off 2 sts, p

*(Continued on page 139)*

# Merry Mobile

for intermediate knitters

Baby will love looking at these country friends from his crib or changing table. Old MacDonald and his farm are knit in simple stitches, accented with embroidery, then suspended from a cleverly painted embroidery hoop. "Merry Mobile" first appeared in the Spring/Summer '98 issue of *Family Circle Easy Knitting* magazine.

## MATERIALS

▦ *Astra* by Patons®, 1³/₄oz/50g skeins, each approx 178yd/163m (acrylic)

*Pig (2)*

   1 skein in #2210 med pink (MC) and small amounts in #2895 dk pink (A) and #2913 brown (C)

*Horse*

   1 skein in #2740 purple (MC) and small amounts in #2941 yellow (A) and #2913 brown (B)

*Sheep*

   1 skein in #2751 white (MC) and small amounts in #2913 brown (A) and #2210 med. pink (B)

*Cat*

   1 skein in #2901 orange (MC) and small amount #2941 yellow (A)

*Man*

   1 skein in #2912 med green (A), #2763 med blue (B), #2751 white (C), #2941 yellow (D) and #2913 brown (E)

   Small amounts in #2901 orange (F) and #2740 purple (G)

*For all*

▦ One pair size 5 (3.75mm) needles OR SIZE TO OBTAIN GAUGE

▦ One set double-pointed needles (dpn) size 5 (3.75mm) for cat only

▦ Size C/2 (2.5mm) crochet hook

▦ Stitch holders

▦ Polyester fiberfill

▦ Tapestry needle

▦ For hanging: one 9"/23cm embroidery hoop

## GAUGE

24 sts and 32 rows to 4"/10cm over St st (unstuffed) using size 5 (3.75mm) needles TAKE TIME TO CHECK YOUR GAUGE.

### Note

Work foll charts for all pieces in St st for first side and reverse St st for second side. Work incs or decs either side of row foll chart. When 2 or more boxes are used in shaping, cast on or bind off sts, joining a new ball of when necessary.

### PIG

(make 2)

**First side**

With A, cast on 6 sts for back leg. Work in St st foll chart for 2 rows, then change to MC and cont foll chart through row 8. Place sts on a holder. With A, cast on 6 sts for front leg and work in same way through row 8.

**Row 9 (RS)** Inc 1 st, work sts of back leg, then cast on 7 sts at beg of front leg to join, work across these sts and front leg sts. Cont to work foll chart, changing colors as indicated, through row 28. Then cont with A only, work in garter st foll chart through row 43. Bind off.

**Second side**

Working in reverse St st instead of St st, work as for first side.

**Tail**

With crochet hook and A, ch 10 firmly. Sc in 2nd ch from hook and in each ch to end. Fasten off.

### FINISHING

Do not block pieces. Sew pieces tog, leaving opening for stuffing. Stuff head. Embroider eye in cross st using C. Sew on tail. Tack ears in place. Finish stuffing and sew final seam.

### HORSE

**First side**

With A, cast on 6 sts for back leg. Work in St st foll chart for 2 rows, then change to MC and cont foll chart through row 14. Place sts on a holder. With A, cast on 6 sts for front leg and work in same way through row 14.

**Row 15 (RS)** Work sts of front leg, then cast on 4 sts at beg of back leg to join, work across these sts and sts of back leg. Cont to foll chart through row 38. Bind off.

### Second side

Working in reverse St st, work as for first side.

FINISHING

Do not block pieces. Sew pieces tog leaving opening for stuffing. Stuff head. With A, embroider mane foll chart. Embroider eyes in cross st using C. With several strands A, make fringe for tail. Finish stuffing and sew final seam.

### SHEEP

### First side

Sheep is worked foll instructions, not a chart.

### PATTERN STITCH

(multiple of 4 sts)

**Row 1 (WS)** *(K1, p1 and k1) into next st, p3tog; rep from * to end.

**Rows 2 and 4** Purl.

**Row 3** *P3tog, (k1, p1 and k1) into next st; rep from * to end.

Rep these 4 rows for pat st.

With MC, cast on 12 sts.

**Row 1 (WS)** Work row 1 of pat st, cast on 4 sts at end—16 sts.

**Row 2** Purl, casting on 4 sts at end—20 sts.

**Row 3** Work row 3 of pat st.

**Row 4** Purl, casting on 4 sts at end—24 sts.

**Row 5** Rep row 1—28 sts. Work even in pat st for 13 more rows.

**Next row** Bind off 4 sts, p to end.

**Next row** Bind off 4 sts, sl last st back to LH needle and work in pat to end. Rep last 2 rows once more. Bind off rem 12 sts.

### Second side

Work as for first side.

### Leg

(Make 4)

With A, cast on 6 sts. Work in St st for 8 rows. Bind off.

### Head

With A, cast on 5 sts. Work 2 rows in St st.

**Next row** K to center st, M1, k1, M1, k to end work 1 row even. Rep last 2 rows twice more—11 st.

**Next row** k1, [k3tog] 3 times, k1. Bind off rem 5 sts.

### FINISHING

Do not block pieces. Sew pieces tog leaving opening for stuffing. Sew on head and legs. Stuff and sew final seam. Embroider eyes in cross st using B.

### CAT

### First side

With MC, cast on 12 sts. Work in St st foll chart through row 41.

### Second side

Work same as first side. (Pieces are identical. It is not necessary to work in reverse St st).

### Tail

With MC and dpn, cast on 4 sts. **Row 1** Knit. Slide sts back to beg of needle and bring yarn around from the back to knit sts again. Rep this row for I-cord for 3"/7.5cm. Bind off.

### FINISHING

Do not block pieces. Sew pieces tog leaving opening for stuffing. Stuff head and embroider face on both sides using A foll chart. Tack tail to side. With MC, embroider legs in stem st. Stuff and sew final seam.

### MAN

### First side

With A, cast on 17 sts. Work in St st foll chart, changing colors as indicated through row 41. Bind off.

### Second side

Work as for first side. (Pieces are identical. It is not necessary to work in reverse St st.)

### FINISHING

Do not block pieces. Sew pieces tog leaving opening for stuffing. Stuff partially. Foll photo, embroider mouth and eyes with B, eyebrows with E, buttons in duplicate st with G and suspenders in stem st with F. Matching colors, embroider through all thicknesses to mark arms and leg division. Finish stuffing and sew final seam.

With crochet hook and matching yarn, make an 11"/28cm chain for hanging each piece for mobile. Make four 16"/40.5cm chains for hanging mobile and gather at top to place on a hook for hanging.

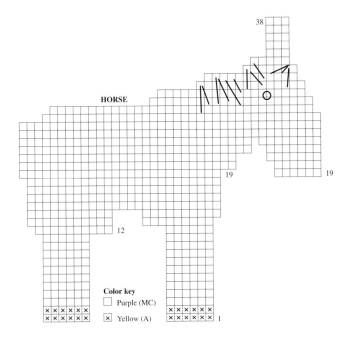

**HORSE**

38

19    19

12

**Color key**
☐ Purple (MC)
☒ Yellow (A)

1

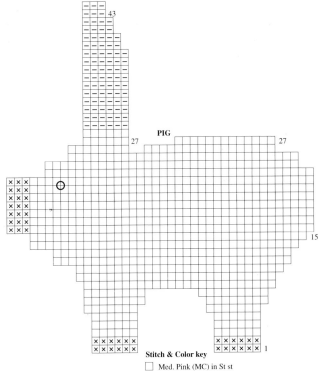

**PIG**

43

27    27

15

1

**Stitch & Color key**
☐ Med. Pink (MC) in St st
☒ Dk. Pink (A) in St st
⊟ Dk. Pink (A) in garter st

**Color key**
◩ Med. Green (A)
· Med. Blue (B)
☐ White (C)
❘ Yellow (D)
✚ Brown (E)
⊙ Purple (G)

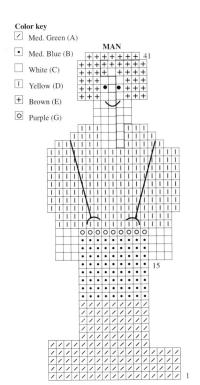

**MAN**

41

15

1

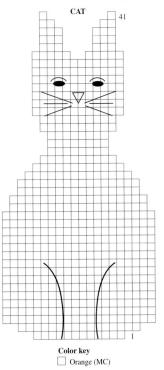

**CAT**

41

1

**Color key**
☐ Orange (MC)

Our fluffy friend is proudly outfitted in his very own cardigan—just in time for Easter! Designed at the Cleckheaton Design Studio, he is stuffed with fiberfill and has an embroidered nose and button eyes. "Hop to It" first appeared in the Spring/Summer '99 issue of *Family Circle Easy Knitting* magazine.

## MATERIALS

*Bunny*

- *Torbellino Mohair* by Cleckheaton/Plymouth Yarns, 1¾oz/50g balls, each approx 97yd/160m (mohair/wool/nylon/acrylic)
  10 balls white(MC)
- *Country 8-Ply* by Cleckheaton/Plymouth Yarns 1¾oz/50g balls, each approx 105yd/96m (wool)
  1 ball #1934 pink(A)
- Polyester fiberfill
- Contrast yarn for embroidery of nose
- 2 purchased eyes or buttons

*Cardigan*

- *Country 8-Ply* by Cleckheaton/Plymouth Yarns
  2 balls in #1935 blue (B)
- Three buttons

*Both*

- One pair each sizes 3 and 6 (3 and 4mm) needles OR SIZE TO OBTAIN GAUGE
- Stitch holder

## FINISHED MEASUREMENTS

*Bunny*

- Chest (approx) 20½"/52cm
- Height (excluding ears) 13¾"/35cm

*Cardigan*

- Chest 20½"/52cm
- Length 5½"/14cm
- Sleeve Length 3½"/9cm

## GAUGES

*Bunny*

- 23 sts and 32 rows to 4"/10cm over St st using smaller needles and MC.

*Cardigan*

- 22 sts and 30 rows to 4"/10cm over St st using larger needles.

TAKE TIME TO CHECK YOUR GAUGES.

## BUNNY

### BODY

(beg at base)

With smaller needles and MC, cast on 20 sts.

**Row 1 (RS)** K2, [inc in next st, k2] 6 times—26 sts.

**Row 2 and all WS rows** Purl.

**Row 3** K2, [inc in next st, k3] 6 times—32 sts.

**Row 5** K3, [inc in next st, k4] 5 times, inc in next st, k3—38 sts.

**Row 7** K3, [inc in next st, k5] 5 times, inc in next st, k4—44 sts.

**Row 9** K4, [inc in next st, k6] 5 times, inc in next st, K4—50 sts.

**Row 11** K4, [inc in next st, k7] 5 times, inc in next st, k5—56 sts.

**Row 13** K5, [inc in next st, k8] 5 times, inc in next st, k5—62 sts.

Cont in this way to inc 6 sts every RS row until there are 92 sts.

Work 59 rows even.

**Row 83** K8, [k2tog, k13] 5 times, k2tog, k7.

**Rows 84 and all foll WS rows** Purl.

**Row 85** K7, [k2tog, k12] 5 times, k2tog, k7.

**Row 87** K7, [k2tog, k11] 5 times, k2tog, k6.

**Row 89** K6, [k2tog, k10] 5 times, k2tog, k6—68 sts.

**Row 91** K2, *k2tog, k1; rep from * to end—46 sts.

Work 1 row even. Bind off.

Run a gathering thread through cast-on sts at lower edge of body, draw up tightly and fasten off securely. Join center back seam of body and fill firmly, leaving neck edge open.

### HEAD

With smaller needles and MC, cast on 45 sts.

Work 4 rows St st.

**Row 5** *K2, inc in next st, k2; rep from * to end—54 sts.

Work 3 rows even.

**Row 9** *K2, inc in next st, k3; rep from * to end—63 sts.

Work 3 rows even.

**Row 13** *K3, inc in next st; k3, rep from * to end—72 sts.

*(Continued on page 141)*

# Baby Knits Basics

The best projects are handmade treasures, stitched with love. As one of the leading authorities in knitwear today, *Family Circle Easy Knitting* proudly presents *Family Circle Easy Baby Knits*, the fourth addition to the best-selling book series. With more than fifty popular knit and crochet designs for babies and toddlers, this expansive collection of classic and contemporary knitwear includes styles from some of the more prominent designers today. From a charming layette set for baby to a circus-inspired pullover for your small fry, there's something to meet every season, occasion and skill level.

Feel free to experiment—now is the time to test out your favorite yarns and colors and try something different. Since these are baby knits, they're meant to be fanciful and fun. You may just end up creating a new texture or color combination that will surprise you.

Your children's measurements are constantly changing during these tender years and we strongly recommend taking your child's measurements before you begin knitting. Whether you're looking for a precious teddy bear dress for your little girl or a sheep-motif diaper bag, you'll find the perfect pattern for your little one in this delightful assortment of unforgettable designs.

## GARMENT CONSTRUCTION

Even though most of the garments in this book are made in pieces, if you are a fairly experienced knitter, you can try knitting many of them in the round, or pick up your sleeve stitches at the shoulder edge and knit down to the cuff. You just need to make some simple adjustments to the pattern.

## SIZING

Since clothing measurements have changed in recent decades, it is important to measure your child to determine which size to make.

## YARN SELECTION

For an exact reproduction of the projects photographed, use the yarn listed in the "Materials" section of the pattern. We've chosen yarns that are readily available in the U.S. and Canada at the time of printing. The Resources list on pages 143 provides addresses of yarn distributors. Contact them for the name of a retailer in your area.

## YARN SUBSTITUTION

You may wish to substitute yarns. Perhaps you view small-scale projects as a chance to incorporate leftovers from your yarn stash, or the yarn specified may not be available in your area. You'll need to knit to the given gauge to obtain the knitted measurements with a substitute yarn (see "Gauge" below). Be sure to consider how the fiber content of the substitute yarn will affect the comfort and the ease of care of your projects.

After you've successfully gauge-swatched a substitute yarn, you'll need to figure out how much of the substitute yarn the project requires. First, find the total length of the original yarn in the pattern (multiply number of balls by yards/meters per ball). Divide this figure by the new yards/meters per ball (listed on the ball band). Round up to the next whole number. The answer is the number of balls required.

## FOLLOWING CHARTS

Charts are a convenient way to follow colorwork, lace, cable, and other stitch patterns at a glance. *FCEK* stitch charts utilize the universal knitting language of "symbolcraft." When knitting back and forth in rows, read charts from right to left on right side (RS) rows and from left to right on wrong side (WS) rows, repeating any stitch and row repeats as directed in the pattern. When knitting in the round, read charts from right to left on every round. Posting a self-adhesive note under your working row is an easy way to keep track of your place on a chart.

## LACE

Lace knitting provides a feminine touch. Knitted lace is formed with "yarn overs," which create an eyelet hole in combination with decreases that create directional effects. To make a yarn over (yo), merely pass the yarn over the right-hand needle to form a new loop. Decreases are worked as k2tog, ssk, or SKP depending on the desired slant and are spelled out specifically with each instruction. On the row or round that follows the lace or eyelet detail, each yarn over is treated as one stitch. If you're new to lace knitting, it's a good idea to count the stitches at the end of each row or round. Making a gauge swatch in the stitch pattern enables you to practice the lace pattern. Instead of binding off the swatch, place the final row on a holder, as the bind off tends to pull in the stitches and distort the gauge.

## COLORWORK KNITTING

Two main types of colorwork are explored in this book.

## INTARSIA

Intarsia is accomplished with separate bobbins of individual colors. This method is ideal for large blocks of color or for motifs that aren't repeated close together. When changing colors, always pick up the new color and wrap it around the old color to prevent holes.

## GAUGE

It is always important to knit a gauge swatch, and it is even more so with garments or they will not fit properly. If your gauge is too loose, you could end up with an over-sized garment, if it's too tight, the garment will be too small. The type of needles used—straight, circular, wood or metal—will influence gauge, so knit your swatch with the needles you plan to use for the project. Measure gauge as illustrated here. (Launder and block your gauge swatch before taking measurements). Try different needle sizes until your sample measures the required number of stitches and rows. To get fewer stitches to the inch/cm, use larger needles; to get more stitches to the inch/cm, use smaller needles. It's a good idea to keep your gauge swatch to test any embroidery or embellishment, as well as blocking, and cleaning methods.

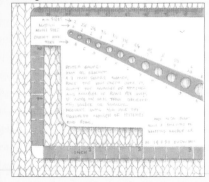

## TWISTED CORD

**1** If you have someone to help you, insert a pencil or knitting needle through each end of the strands. If not, place one end over a doorknob and put a pencil through the other end. Turn the strands clockwise until they are tightly twisted.

**2** Keeping the strands taut, fold the piece in half. Remove the pencils and allow the cords to twist onto themselves.

## STRANDING

When motifs are closely placed, colorwork is accomplished by stranding along two or more colors per row, creating "floats" on the wrong side of the fabric. This technique is sometimes called Fair Isle knitting after the traditional Fair Isle patterns that are composed of small motifs with frequent color changes.

To keep an even tension and prevent holes while knitting, pick up yarns alternately over and under one another across or around. While knitting, stretch the stitches on the needle slightly wider than the length of the float at the back to keep work from puckering.

When changing colors at the beginning of rows or rounds, carry yarn along for a few rows only, or cut yarn and rejoin when needed. It is important to keep the "floats" small and neat so they don't catch when pulling on the piece.

## BLOCKING

Blocking is an all-important finishing step in the knitting process. It is the best way to shape pattern pieces and smooth knitted edges in preparation for sewing together. Most garments retain their shape if the blocking stages in the instructions are followed carefully. Choose a blocking method according to the yarn care label and when in doubt, test-block your gauge swatch.

## WET BLOCK METHOD

Using rust-proof pins, pin pieces to measurements on a flat surface and lightly dampen using a spray bottle. Allow to dry before removing pins.

## STEAM BLOCK METHOD

With WS facing, pin pieces. Steam lightly, holding the iron 2"/5cm above the knitting. Do not press or it will flatten stitches.

## FINISHING

The pieces in this book use a variety of finishing techniques. Directions for making fringes and tassels are on page 118. Also refer to the illustrations such as "Invisible Seaming: Stockinette St" for other useful techniques.

## HAND-SEWING

Several items in this book require hand-sewing in the finishing. Use a fine point handsewing needle and sewing thread that matches the color of the trim. Cut the unsewn ends at an angle to prevent unraveling. When sewing on a trim, use back stitch and keep the stitches small and even.

## CARE

Refer to the yarn label for the recommended cleaning method. Many of the projects in the book can be either washed by hand, or in the machine on a gentle or wool cycle, in lukewarm water with a mild detergent. Do not agitate, or soak for more than 10 minutes. Rinse gently with tepid water, then fold in a towel and gently press the water out. Lay flat to dry away from excess heat and light. Check the yarn band for any specific care instructions such as dry cleaning or tumble drying.

## INVISIBLE SEAMING: STOCKINETTE ST

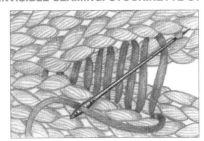

To make an invisible side seam in a garment worked in stockinette stitch, insert the tapestry needle under the horizontal bar between the first and second stitches. Insert the needle into the corresponding bar on the other piece. Pull the yarn gently until the sides meet. Continue alternating from side to side.

## CROCHET STITCHES

**CHAIN**
**1** Pass the yarn over the hook and catch it with the hook.

**2** Draw the yarn through the loop on the hook.

**3** Repeat steps 1 and 2 to make a chain.

**SINGLE CROCHET**
**1** Insert the hook through top two loops of a stitch. Pass the yarn over the hook and draw up a loop—two loops on hook.

**2** Pass the yarn over the hook and draw through both loops on hook.

**3** Continue in the same way, inserting the hook into each stitch.

## DUPLICATE STITCH

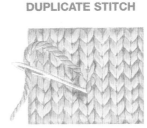 

Duplicate stitch covers a knit stitch. Bring the needle up below the stitch to be worked. Insert the needle under both loops one row above and pull it through. Insert it back into the stitch below and through the center of the next stitch in one motion, as shown.

## POMPOMS

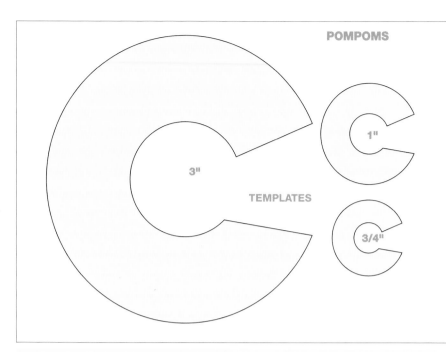

TEMPLATES

**1** Following the template, cut two circular pieces of cardboard.

**2** Hold the two circles together and wrap the yarn tightly around the cardboard several times. Secure and carefully cut the yarn.

**3** Tie a piece of yarn tightly between the two circles. Remove the cardboard and trim the pompom to the desired size.

## EMBROIDERY STITCHES

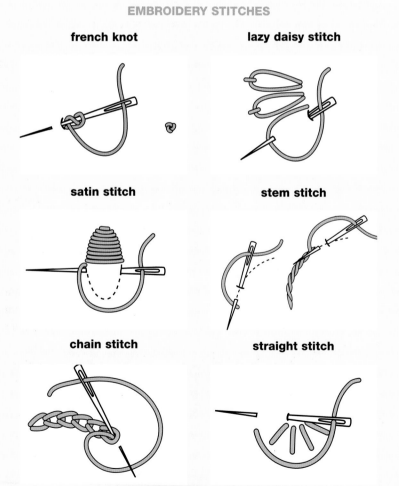

**french knot**

**lazy daisy stitch**

**satin stitch**

**stem stitch**

**chain stitch**

**straight stitch**

## TASSELS

Cut a piece of cardboard to the desired length of the tassel. Wrap yarn around the cardboard. Knot a piece of yarn tightly around one end, cut as shown, and remove the cardboard. Wrap and tie yarn around the tassel about 1"/2.5cm down from the top to secure the fringe.

## FRINGE

**Simple fringe:** Cut yarn twice desired length plus extra for knotting. On wrong side, insert hook from front to back through piece and over folded yarn. Pull yarn through. Draw ends through and tighten. Trim yarn.

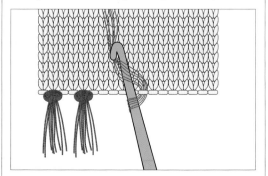

# Knit/Crochet Terms and Abbreviations

approx  approximately

beg  begin(ning)

bind off  Used to finish an edge and keep stitches from unraveling. Lift the first stitch over the second, the second over the third, etc. (UK: cast off)

cast on  A foundation row of stitches placed on the needle in order to begin knitting.

CC  contrast color

ch  chain(s)

cm  centimeter(s)

cont  continu(e)(ing)

dc  double crochet (UK: tr–treble)

dec  decrease(ing)–Reduce the stitches in a row (knit 2 together).

dpn  double-pointed needle(s)

dtr  double treble (UK: trtr—triple treble)

foll  follow(s)(ing)

g  gram(s)

garter stitch  Knit every row. Circular knitting: knit one round, then purl one round.

grp(s)  group(s)

hdc  half double crochet (UK: htr–half treble)

inc  increase(ing)–Add stitches in a row (knit into the front and back of a stitch).

k  knit

k2tog  knit 2 stitches together

LH  left-hand

lp(s)  loop(s)

m  meter(s)

M1  make one stitch–With the needle tip, lift the strand between last stitch worked and next stitch on the left-hand needle and knit into the back of it. One stitch has been added.

MC  main color

mm  millimeter(s)

no stitch  On some charts, "no stitch" is indicated with shaded spaces where stitches have been decreased or not yet made. In such cases, work the stitches of the chart, skipping over the "no stitch" spaces.

oz  ounce(s)

p  purl

p2tog  purl 2 stitches together

pat(s)  pattern

pick up and knit (purl)  Knit (or purl) into the loops along an edge.

pm  place markers–Place or attach a loop of contrast yarn or purchased stitch marker as indicated.

psso  pass slip stitch(es) over

rem  remain(s)(ing)

rep  repeat

rev St st  reverse stockinette stitch–Purl right-side rows, knit wrong-side rows. Circular knitting: purl all rounds. (UK: reverse stocking stitch)

rnd(s)  round(s)

RH  right-hand

RS  right side(s)

sc  single crochet (UK: dc–double crochet)

sk  skip

SKP  Slip 1, knit 1, pass slip stitch over knit 1.

SK2P  Slip 1, knit 2 together, pass slip stitch over the knit 2 together.

sl  slip–An unworked stitch made by passing a stitch from the left-hand to the right-hand needle as if to purl.

sl st  slip stitch (UK: sc–single crochet)

sp(s)  space(s)

ssk  slip, slip, knit–Slip next 2 stitches knitwise, one at a time, to right-hand needle. Insert tip of left-hand needle into fronts of these stitches from left to right. Knit them together. One stitch has been decreased.

sssk  Slip next 3 sts knitwise, one at a time, to right-hand needle. Insert tip of left-hand needle into fronts of these stitches from left to right. Knit them together. Two stitches have been decreased.

st(s)  stitch(es)

St st  Stockinette stitch–Knit right-side rows, purl wrong-side rows. Circular knitting: knit all rounds. (UK: stocking stitch)

tbl  through back of loop

t-ch  turning chain

tog  together

tr  treble (UK: dtr—double treble)

trtr  triple treble (UK: qtr—quadruple treble)

WS  wrong side(s)

wyib  with yarn in back

wyif  with yarn in front

work even  Continue in pattern without increasing or decreasing. (UK: work straight)

yd  yard(s)

yo  yarn over–Make a new stitch by wrapping the yarn over the right-hand needle. (UK: yfwd, yon, yrn)

* = Repeat directions following * as many times as indicated.

[ ] = Repeat directions inside brackets as many times as indicated.

| KNITTING NEEDLES | | CROCHET HOOKS | |
| --- | --- | --- | --- |
| US | METRIC | US | METRIC |
| 0 | 2mm | 14 steel | .60mm |
| 1 | 2.25mm | 12 steel | .75mm |
| 2 | 2.5mm | 10 steel | 1.00mm |
| 3 | 3mm | 6 steel | 1.50mm |
| 4 | 3.5mm | | |
| 5 | 3.75mm | 5 steel | 1.75mm |
| 6 | 4mm | B/1 | 2.00mm |
| 7 | 4.5mm | C/2 | 2.50mm |
| 8 | 5mm | D/3 | 3.00mm |
| 9 | 5.5mm | E/4 | 3.50mm |
| 10 | 6mm | F/5 | 4.00mm |
| 10½ | 6.5, 7, 7.5mm | G/6 | 4.50mm |
| 11 | 8mm | H/8 | 5.00mm |
| 13 | 9mm | I/9 | 5.50mm |
| 15 | 10mm | J/10 | 6.00mm |
| 17 | 12.75mm | | |
| 19 | 16mm | | 6.50mm |
| 35 | 19mm | K/10½ | 7.00mm |

# Sugar and Spice

GO FISH

*(Continued from page 14)*

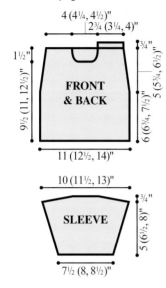

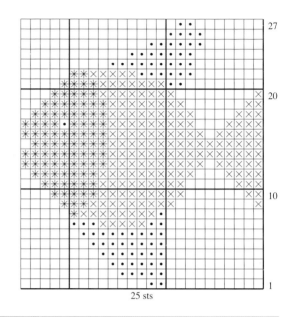

**Color Key**

| White Version | Green Version |
|---|---|
| ☐ White (MC) | ☐ Green (MC) |
| ⊙ Green (A) | ⊙ White (A) |
| ✳ Dk blue (B) | ✳ Med blue (B) |
| ⊠ Med blue (C) | ⊠ Dk blue (C) |

25 sts

## PATCHWORK PLEASER

*(Continued from page 16)*

### Neck shaping

**Next row (RS)** Work in pat over 18 (18, 19) sts, join 2nd ball of yarn and bind off center 15 (17, 17) sts, work to end. Working both sides at once, dec 1 st at each neck edge every other row twice—16 (16, 18) sts each side. Work even until armhole measures 4½ (5, 5½)"/10 (13, 14)cm.

### Shoulder shaping

Bind off 5 (5, 6) sts at beg of next 4 rows, 6 sts at beg of next 2 rows.

### BACK

Work as for front until first row of bodice has been worked—63 (67, 71) sts.

### Bodice

**Next row (WS)** P 30 (32, 34) sts, place sts on holder (for left bodice).

### Right bodice

Join 2nd ball of yarn and bind off center 3 sts, cast on 6 sts, p rem 30 (32, 34) sts—36 (38, 40) sts. **Next row (RS)** Work in Knot st pat as for front to last 6 sts, (k1, p1) 3 times for buttonband. **Next row (WS)** (K1, p1) 3 times, complete row in Knot st pat. Rep last 2 rows until 1½"/4cm from beg of bodice. Cont buttonband rib and shape armhole as for front—22 (22, 26) sts.

When same length as front armhole, bind off at armhole edge 5 (5, 6) sts twice, bind off rem sts for back neck. Place markers for 4 buttons evenly spaced along buttonband.

### Left bodice

With A, cast on 6 sts for buttonhole band, pick up and work in pat across left bodice sts on holder—36 (38, 40) sts. Work to correspond to right bodice, reversing armhole and shoulder shaping and working buttonholes (bind off 2 center sts on RS row and cast on 2 sts on next row) in band to match markers on right bodice. Embroider lazy daisy flowers in blocks as shown. Duplicate st eyes and nose on bear motifs and embroider mouth with stem stitch.

### Scallop Border

With smaller needles, work 2 scallops each of B, H, I, D, G, and 4 scallops each of E, F, C (8 of these scallops are used for hat). With A, pick up and k across sts of each of 11 scallops in color sequence as shown to join into a border. Bind off. Sew border to top of garter hem at bottom of each skirt.

### SLEEVES

With smaller needles and A, cast on 38 sts. Work in St st for 1"/2.5cm, then inc 1 st each side every 4th (2nd, 4th) row 10 (11, 12) times —58

(60, 62) sts. Work even until 8½ (9, 9½)"/21.5 (23, 24)cm from beg. Bind off 4 (5, 6) sts beg of 2 rows, 2 sts at beg of 2 rows, dec 1 st each end every other row 8 times—30 sts. Bind off 3 sts at beg of 6 rows, bind off rem 12 sts.

### FINISHING

Block pieces to measurements. Sew shoulder seams. With smaller needles and A, pick up and k 71 (75, 75) sts along entire neck edge. Cont in St st for 1"/2.5cm. Bind off. Sew in sleeves. Sew side and sleeve seams. Sew on buttons.

### HAT

With smaller needles and A, cast on 83 sts. K 12 rows. Beg with K row, work in St st for 4 rows. **Next row (RS)** K over 31 sts for knot st pat, k 21 sts of Chart #3, k over last 31 sts for Knot st pat. Cont in pats as established with G, H, E, B, C, F, D for color stripes of knot st, and use C for MC and D for bear motif of Chart #3. Cont to top of chart, then work even in knot st pat on all sts for 1"/2.5cm, end with WS row. **Next row (RS)** K2 tog across. P WS row. **Next row (RS)** K2 tog across. Cut yarn, lace yarn end through sts of last row, pull to close and secure. Use A to join rem scallops into border and sew to top of garter st edge. Duplicate stitch bear motif and embroider mouth with stem stitch. Sew hat seam.

*(Continued from page 120)*

**Tassels**

(make 1 each D, E, G)

With smaller needles, cast on 30 sts. **Row 1** * K in front and back of next st; rep from *—60 sts. Bind off all sts. Allow sts to twist into corkscrew shape. Sew one end of each tassel to center top of hat.

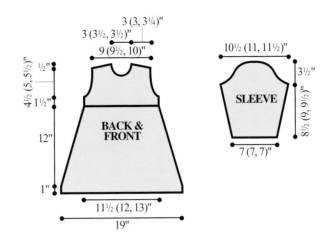

Chart 1

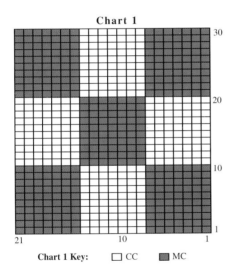

Chart 1 Key:     □ CC     ■ MC

Chart 2

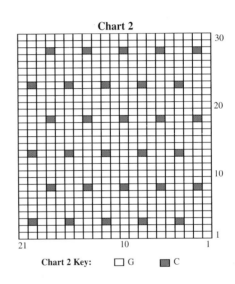

Chart 2 Key:     □ G     ■ C

Chart 3

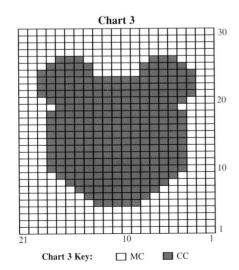

Chart 3 Key:     □ MC     ■ CC

Chart 4

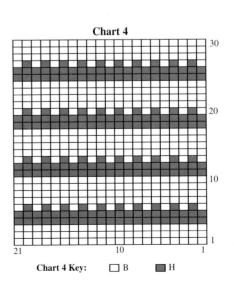

Chart 4 Key:     □ B     ■ H

*(Continued from page 18)*

instructions or chart), inc 1 st each side (working inc sts into pat) every 4th row 10 (14, 16) times—71 (79, 83) sts. Work even until piece measures 6 (7, 8½)"/15 (17.5, 21.5)cm from beg. Bind off.

### FINISHING

Block pieces to measurements. Embroider motifs on front with duplicate st as shown in photo, or as desired. Sew right shoulder seam.

**Neckband**

With RS facing, smaller needles and A, beg at left front neck, pick up and k 79 (79, 85) sts evenly around neck edge. Work in rib/lace pat for 9 rows. Bind off in rib.

Tack left shoulder seam. Place markers at 4¾ (4½, 5)"/12 (13.5, 14)cm down from shoulders. Sew sleeves to armholes between markers. Sew side and sleeve seams. Sew 2 buttons on button flap and 1 button on back neckband (the yo in the lace/rib pat serves as a buttonhole).

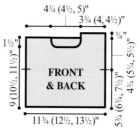

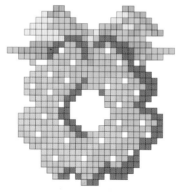

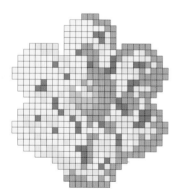

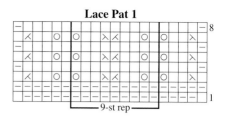

**Lace Pat 1**

9-st rep

**Lace Pat 2**

6-st rep

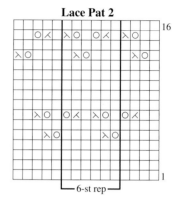

### Stitch Key

☐ K on RS, p on WS

⊟ P on RS, k on WS

⊡ Yo

⊠ K2tog

⊠ SKP

### Color Key

| | | | |
|---|---|---|---|
| ▨ Carmel 365 | ▨ Dk. pink 11 | ▨ Dk. beige 901 | ▨ Dk. orange 324 |
| ▨ Lt. carmel 363 | ▨ Champagne 361 | ☐ Lt. yellow 301 | ☐ Pale pink 6 |
| ☐ Yellow 295 | ☐ Lt. yellow 292 | ▨ Beige 891 | ☐ Ivory 386 |
| ▨ Grey 398 | ▨ Dk. rose 54 | ▨ Brown beige 379 | ▨ Dk. pale brown 375 |
| ☐ White 1 | ▨ Rose 52 | ☐ Lt. brown beige 376 | ▨ Pale brown 373 |
| ▨ Red 9046 | ☐ Lt. rose 50 | ▨ Orange 323 | ▨ Dk. pink 9 |

(Continued from page 20)

and sleeve seams. Fold band at lower edge of body and sleeves to WS at eyelet row and sew in place.

Sew on buttons.

## VEST

### FINISHED MEASUREMENTS

■ Chest (buttoned) 20 (21½, 23)"/50.5 (54.5, 58.5)cm

■ Length 7¼ (7½, 8)"/18 (19, 20)cm

### GAUGE

25 sts and 34 rows to 4"/10cm over St st using larger needles.

TAKE TIME TO CHECK YOUR GAUGE.

### Note

All measurements on schematics reflect the measurement "above" the eyelet row.

### STRIPE PATTERN

*6 rows CC, 6 rows MC; rep from * (12 rows) for stripe pat.

### BACK

With smaller needles and MC, cast on 63 (67, 73) sts. P 1 row, k 1 row, p 1 row. **Eyelet Row (RS)** *K2tog, yo; rep from *, end k1. Work 3 rows in St st. Change to larger needles. Work 2 rows St st, 2 rows garter st, 4 rows St st.

### Beg heart chart

**Row 1 (RS)** Beg with st 1 (3, 4), work to st 11, work 8-st rep 6 (7, 8) times, end with st 15 (13, 12). Cont in pat as established through row 6. With MC, work 4 rows St st, 2 rows garter st. Cont in St st and stripe pat until piece measures 2½"/6cm above eyelet row.

### Armhole shaping

Bind off 3 sts at beg of next 2 rows, 2 sts at beg of next 4 rows. Dec 1 st each side every other row 3 times—43 (47, 53) sts. Work even until armhole measures 4½ (4¾, 5¼)"/11 (12, 13)cm, end with a WS row.

### Neck shaping

**Next row (RS)** Work 13 (14, 17) sts, join 2nd ball of yarn and bind off center 17 (19, 19) sts, work to end. Working both sides at once with separate balls of yarn, bind off 3 sts from each neck edge once. When armhole measures 4¾ (5, 5½)"/12 (13, 14)cm, bind off rem 10 (11, 14)

sts each side for shoulders.

### LEFT FRONT

With smaller needles and MC, cast on 59 (63, 69) sts. Work as for back, beg heart chart same as for back and end with st 11(9, 8), until piece measures 2"/5cm above eyelet row, end with a WS row.

### Neck shaping

**Next row (RS)** Work to last 4 sts, k3tog, k1. Cont to dec 2 st at neck edge every other row 16 (17, 19) times more, then dec 1 st at neck edge (working k2tog instead of k3tog) every other row 5 (6, 5) times, AT SAME TIME, when same length as back to armhole, shape armhole at side edge only (beg of RS rows) as for back. When piece measures same as back, bind off rem 10 (11, 14) sts for shoulder.

### RIGHT FRONT

Work to correspond to left front, reversing chart pat by beg with st 5 (7, 8) and ending as for back. Reverse all shaping working SK2P instead of K3tog and SKP instead of K2tog for neck shaping.

### FINISHING

Block pieces to measurements. Sew shoulder seams.

### Armhole bands

With RS facing, smaller needles and MC, pick up and k 67 (71, 75) sts evenly around each armhole edge. K 1 row on WS, then work in St st for 4 rows. Work eyelet row as for back, then work 5 more rows in St st. Bind off. Fold band in half to WS at eyelet row and sew in place.

### Front band

With RS facing, smaller needles and MC, pick up and k 145 (151, 157) sts evenly along right front, back neck and left front edges. K 1 row on WS. Work in St st for 2 rows. **Next (buttonhole) row (RS)** K4, bind off 2 sts, k5, bind off 2 sts, work to end. P next row, casting on 2 sts over bound off sts. Work eyelet row as for back, then work 1 row in St st. Work 2 more buttonholes over next 2 rows. Work 2 more rows in St st. Bind off. Fold band in half to WS at eyelet row and sew in place.

Sew side seams. Fold band at lower edge to WS at eyelet row and sew in place. Sew two

buttons to left front opposite buttonholes. Make a button loop at left front edge above eyelet band. Sew button to WS of right front opposite loop.

PULLOVER

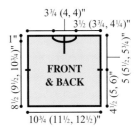

**Polka Dot Chart**

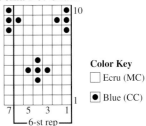

Color Key
☐ Ecru (MC)
● Blue (CC)

VEST

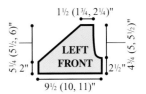

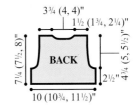

**Heart Chart**

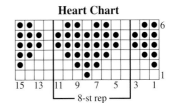

Color Key
☐ Ecru (MC)
● Blue (CC)

## BEACH BABE

*(Continued from page 22)*

15 (17, 19) sts. Work even until armhole measures 2½ (3, 3½)"/6.5 (7.5, 9)cm.

### Neck shaping

**Next row (RS)** Bind off 4 (4, 6) sts, work to end. Cont to bind off from neck edge 3 sts 1 (2, 2) times, then dec 1 st every other row 2 (1, 1) time, AT SAME TIME, when armhole measures 3 (3½, 4)"/7.5 (9, 10)cm, bind off 2 sts from armhole edge every other row 3 times.

### RIGHT BACK

Work to correspond to left back reversing shaping and working first section with B and 2nd section with MC.

### FINISHING

Block pieces to measurements.

### Back buttonhole band

With MC, pick up and k 36 (39, 42) sts along left back edge. Work in garter st for 2 rows. **Next row (WS)** *K9 (10, 11), k2tog, yo; rep from * twice more, k3. K2 rows more. Bind off. Work button band on right back edge to correspond, omitting buttonholes. Sew bands in

place overlapping buttonhole over button band and sewing down to 2-st bind-off. Sew shoulder seams.

### Neckband

With MC, pick up and k 13 (15, 17) sts from right back neck edge (including band), 38 (42, 44) sts along front neck edge and 13 (15, 17) sts along left back neck edge—64 (72, 78) sts. Work in garter st for 1 row. **Next row** K2, yo, k2tog (for buttonhole), k to end. K2 rows. Bind off.

### ARMBANDS

With MC, pick up and k 46 (50, 54) sts along armhole edge. Work in garter st for 5 rows. Bind off. Sew center seams, side and leg seams. Sew on buttons.

### HAT

With MC, cast on 138 (144, 150) sts. Work 5 rows in garter st. **Next row (RS)** *With MC, k23 (24, 25), with A, k23 (24, 25), with B, k23 (24, 25); rep from * once more. Work 1 row even. **Next dec row (RS)** *SKP, k to last 2 sts in MC, k2tog; SKP, k to last 2 sts in A, k2tog; SKP, k to last 2 sts

in B, k2tog; rep from * once more—126 (132, 138) sts. Work 1 row even. Rep last 2 rows 3 times more—90 (96, 102) sts. Work even until piece measures 4 (5, 5½)"/10 (12.5, 14)cm from beg. **Next row (RS)** Rep dec row—12 sts dec'd and 78 (84, 90) sts rem. Work 3 rows even. Rep last 4 rows 4 (5, 5) times more—18 (12, 18) sts rem. For sizes 6 and 18 months ONLY—**Next row (RS)** [K1, k2tog] 6 times—12 sts. Work 1 row even on 12 sts for all sizes. **Next row** [K2tog] 6 times. Cut yarn leaving end for sewing. Draw through all sts and pull tightly to secure. Sew back seam. Block lightly.

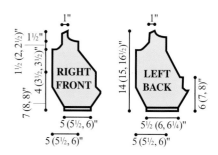

---

## ROMPER ROOM

*(Continued from page 26)*

### Leg bands

With smaller needles and MC, cast on 7 sts for buttonhole band. Work 10 rows in k1, p1 rib.

### Buttonhole row

Rib 3 sts, yo, k2tog, rib 2 sts. Work 13 rows in rib. Rep last 14 rows 3 times more. Rep buttonhole row. Work 10 rows in rib. Bind off in rib. Work a button band in same way omitting buttonholes. Sew button band along back leg opening and buttonhole band along front leg opening.

### Back bands

With smaller needles and MC, cast on 7 sts. Work in k1, p1 rib for 8 rows. Work buttonhole row as on leg band. Work 11 rows in rib. Rep last 12 rows twice more. Work buttonhole row.

With 3 rows in rib, bind off. Work button band in same way, omitting buttonholes. Sew button band to left back and sew buttonhole band to right back, overlapping at opening.

### FINISHING

Block pieces to measurements. Sew shoulder seams.

### Left collar

Place marker at center front neck. With smaller needles and MC, pick up and k 16 sts for back neck (including band), 23 sts to center front neck—39 sts. Work in k1, p1 rib for 2"/5cm. Bind off in rib. Work right collar in same way, beg at center front neck. Sew sleeves into armholes. Sew side and sleeve seams and sew both sides of foot seams. Sew on buttons.

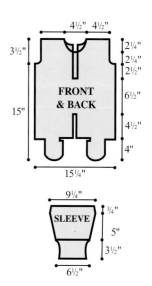

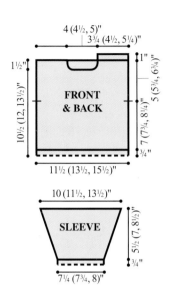

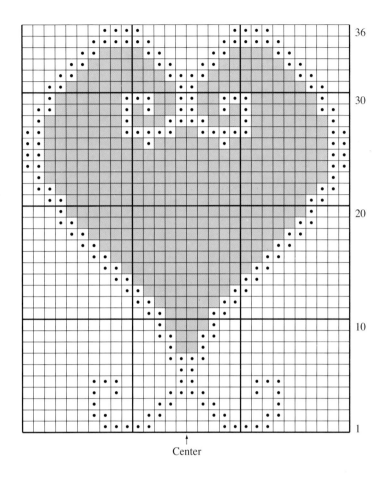

Color Key

☐ MC

▨ A

⊡ B

Center

---

## CROP DUSTER

*(Continued from page 32)*

row twice. Work even through last row of rib on stripe pat.

**Button flap**

With C, cont on 9 sts each side for 3 rows. **Next row** Work 3 sts, yo, k2tog, work to end. Cont in St st, dec 1 st each side every row until 1 st rem. Fasten off st each side.

### POCKET

With straight needles and C, cast on 20 (20, 22)

sts. Work in St st for 3"/7.5cm. Work in k2, p2 rib for 4 rows. Bind off in rib.

FINISHING

Block to measurements. Sew crotch seam. Sew buttons to front shoulder straps. Attach pocket to left front. Decorate pocket with desired buttons (see photo for inspiration).

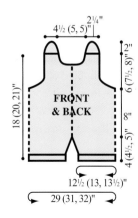

40, 40) sts. Work in Seed st and AT SAME TIME, inc 1 st each side every 6th row 0 (10, 11, 13) times and every 8th row 7 (0, 0, 0) times—50 (56, 62, 66) sts. Work even in pat until piece measures 6 (6½, 7¼, 8)"/15 (16.5, 18.5, 20.5) cm from beg. Bind off all sts.

### FINISHING

Block pieces to measurements. Sew in pocket linings in place. Sew shoulder seams. Mark 4½ (5, 5½, 6)"/11 (13, 14, 15) cm down sides from shoulders for armholes. Sew sleeves between markers. Sew side and sleeve seams.

### Sleeve border

With RS facing, join MC with a sl st at seam. Work 4 rnds of sc. Fasten off.

### Pocket border

With WS facing, join MC with sl st at left end pocket opening, ch 1, sc across—16 (16, 17, 18) sts. Turn. Work 3 more rows sc. Fasten off. Sew ends of pocket border to front.

### Body border

With RS facing, join MC with sl st in lower left front corner, ch 1.

**Rnd 1** Work evenly across edges and work 3 sc in corners and at beg of neck edges sc around, join with a sl st. On left front, mark for 5 buttonholes; first one between 2nd and 3rd sts down from corner st, last one between 2nd and 3rd up from corner st and 3 more evenly spaced between.

**Rnd 2** Cont working 3 sts into corner sts, sc around and (ch 4 -sk 4) sts over each marker, join.

**Rnd 3** Work around as established, working 4 sc in each 4-ch-sp, join. Rep rnd 1 once more, dec 4 sc evenly spaced along neck edge. Fasten off.

### BUTTONS

With MC and crochet hook, ch 5 loosely, join with a sl st to form a chain ring. Place elastic ring over with, with loop at front and yarn

behind. Ch 1 and work 10 sc into center of ring covering plastic ring, join with a sl st. Leaving a tail, fasten off.

### COLLAR

With WS facing, using CC and crochet hook, join with a sl st about ½"/1.5cm from neck edge.

**Row 1** Ch 3 (counts a 1 dc and 1 ch). *sk 1 sc, dc in next sc, dc in next sc, ch 1; rep from *, end with sk 1 sc, dc in next sc and at ½"/1.5cm from right neck corner; turn.

**Row 2** Ch 2 (counts as 1 dc). dc 2 more in 1 ch sp, *ch 1, 3 dc in next ch-sp; rep from *; turn.

**Row 3** Ch 2 (counts as 1 dc and 1 ch), sk 2, *dc 3 in next ch 1 sp, ch 2, sk 3; rep from *, end 3dc, ch 1, sk last 2 sts, dc 1 in 2nd ch of ch 2 in previous row. Fasten off.

### Picot edge

With RS of collar facing, beg at left side, join CC with a sl st,*sc 3, ch 3, sc into first ch of 3 ch- picot; rep from * along edges of collar. Fasten off.

### HAT

With MC and size 6 (4mm) needles, cast on 66 (71, 76, 81) sts. Work in St st for 1"/2.5cm. Cont in Seed st until piece measures 4 (4½, 5, 5½)"/10 (11.5, 12.5, 14)cm from beg (with edge rolled), end with a WS row.

**Next row (RS)** Cont in pat, sl-s dec, *work next 10 (11, 12, 13) sts, sdv dec; rep from * 3 times more, work next 10 (11, 12, 13) sts sr-s dec.

**Next row (WS)** Sl-s dec, *work next 8 (9, 10, 11) sts, sdv dec; rep from * 3 times more. Work next 8 (9, 10, 11) sts sr-s dec. working 2 sts less between decs on every row, cont dec over decs of previous row until there is 0 (1, 0, 1) st left between decs. Leaving a long tail, pull yarn through rem 8 (13, 8, 13) sts. Work seams with invisible vertical seam tog (inserting into center of first dec line at both edge of work) to create the 5th line vertical st.

### Flower

With CC and crochet hook, ch 5, join with a sl st to form a ring.

**Rnd 1** Ch1, work 10 sc into center of ring, join with a sl st.

**Rnd 2** Ch 1,* sc l in next st, (dc 1-tr 1-dc 1) in next st; rep from * around, join with a sl st. Leave a tail and fasten off.

### Leaf

(Work in rounds and half rnds) With CC and crochet hook, ch 7.

**Rnd 1** Insert hook into 2nd ch from hook and working 1 sc into each ch, sc 5, work 3 sc into last ch then cont working 1 sc into each ch along lower side of beg ch, sc 5, work 3 sc into last ch of beg ch. **Rnd 2** Sc into next 4 sts, ch 2; turn. **Rnd 3** Sc into next 5 sts, sc 3 into corner st, sc into next 5 sts, ch 2; turn. **Rnd 4** Sc into next 6 sts, sl st into next st, ch 2. Leaving a tail, fasten off.

### FINISHING

Sew on buttons and appliqués.

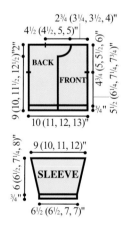

# The Boy's Club

## CABLE CLASSICS

*(Continued from page 36)*

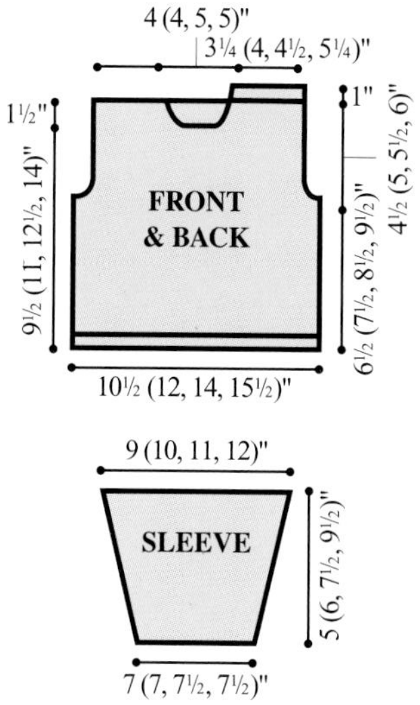

4 (4, 5, 5)"
3¼ (4, 4½, 5¼)"
1½"
1"
FRONT & BACK
9½ (11, 12½, 14)"
6½ (7½, 8½, 9½)"
4½ (5, 5½, 6)"
10½ (12, 14, 15½)"
9 (10, 11, 12)"
SLEEVE
5 (6, 7½, 9½)"
7 (7, 7½, 7½)"


## CREAM OF THE CROP

*(Continued from page 38)*

**Neckband**

With RS facing and MC, pick up and k 64 (68, 72) sts evenly around neck edge and work in garter st for 4 rows. Bind off.

Set in sleeves, sewing last ½"/1.5cm at top of sleeve to bound-off armhole sts. Sew inside leg, side and sleeve seams. Sew on buttons. Fold 1¼"/3cm at lower edge of legs and sleeves to outside for cuffs.

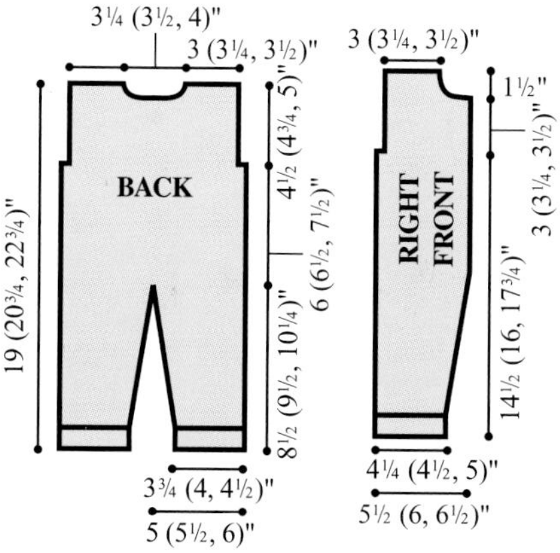

3¼ (3½, 4)"
3 (3¼, 3½)"
BACK
19 (20¾, 22¾)"
4½ (4¾, 5)"
6 (6½, 7½)"
8½ (9½, 10¼)"
3¾ (4, 4½)"
5 (5½, 6)"
3 (3¼, 3½)"
1½"
RIGHT FRONT
3 (3¼, 3½)"
14½ (16, 17¾)"
4¼ (4½, 5)"
5½ (6, 6½)"


## SPRINGTIME FUN

*(Continued from page 42)*

**Shape toe**

Cont with A only as foll: Next rnd K to last 3 sts on needle 1, k2tog, k1; k1, SKP, k to last 3 sts, k2tog, k1 on needle 2; k1, SKP k to end on needle 3. Work 1 rnd even. Rep these 2 rnds twice more—18 sts rem. Divide sts onto 2 needles and weave toe sts tog using Kitchener st.

### PULLOVER

### FINISHED MEASUREMENTS

- Chest 20 (22, 24)"/51 (56, 61)cm
- Length 10 (11, 12)"/25.5 (28, 30.5)cm
- Upper arm 9 (9½, 10½)"/23 (24, 27)cm

### GAUGE

24 sts and 28 rows to 4"/10cm over St st using larger needles.
TAKE TIME TO CHECK YOUR GAUGE.

### BACK

With smaller needles and CC, cast on 60 (66, 72) sts.

**Row 1 (RS)** *K1, p1; rep from * to end.

**Row 2** K the purl and p the knit sts. Rep row 2 for seed st pat for ½"/1.5cm. Change to larger needles and cont with MC in St st until piece measures 10 (11, 12)"/25.5 (28, 30.5)cm from beg.

**Next row (RS)** Bind off 18 (21, 24) sts for right shoulder, work 24 sts and place on holder for neck, work rem 18 (21, 24) sts and place on holder for left shoulder.

### FRONT

Work as for back until piece measures 8 (9, 10)"/20.5 (23, 25.5)cm from beg.

**Neck shaping**

**Next row (RS)** K24 (27, 30), join another ball of yarn and k 12 sts and sl to a holder for neck, k to end. Cont to work both sides at once, bind off 2 sts from each neck edge twice, dec 1 st each side every other row twice—18 (21, 24) sts rem each side. Cont each side until piece measures 9¼ (10¼, 11¼)"/23.5 (26, 28.5)cm from beg. Place left shoulder sts on a holder and work right shoulder to same length as back.

### SLEEVES

With smaller needles and CC, cast on 42 (44, 46) sts. Work in seed st pat for ½"/1.5cm. Change to larger needles and cont with MC in St st inc 1 st each side every other row 6 (7, 8) times—54 (58, 62) sts. Work even until piece measures 2½ (2¾, 3)"/6.5 (7, 7.5)cm from beg. Bind off.

### FINISHING

Block pieces to measurements. Sew right shoulder seam.

**Neckband**

With smaller needles and CC, pick up and k 60 sts evenly around neck edge. Work in seed st for ½"/1.5cm. Bind off.

**Left shoulder button band**

With smaller needles and CC, pick up and k 5 sts from side of back neckband, then work in seed st across 18 (21, 24) sts from holder for left shoulder. Work in seed st for ½"/1.5cm. Bind off.

**Buttonhole band**

Work as for buttonband working row 2 as foll:

**Row 2** Work 3 (3, 4) sts, *k2tog, yo, k6 (7, 8); rep from * once, k2tog, yo, work 2 (3, 3) sts. Sew on buttons opposite buttonholes and button closed. Place markers at 4½ (4¾, 5¼)"/11.5 (12, 13.5)cm down from shoulders. Sew left sleeve to armhole edge with band closed. Sew other sleeve to armhole. Sew side and sleeve seams.

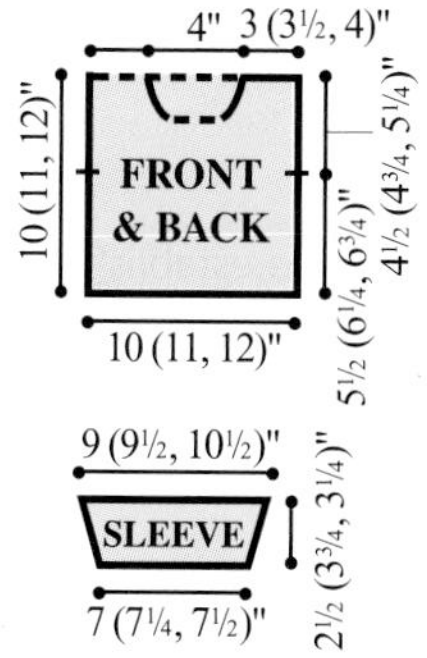

4"
3 (3½, 4)"
FRONT & BACK
10 (11, 12)"
4½ (4¾, 5¼)"
5½ (6¼, 6¾)"
10 (11, 12)"
9 (9½, 10½)"
SLEEVE
2½ (3¾, 3¼)"
7 (7¼, 7½)"

## WHALE OF A TIME

*(Continued from page 40)*

### Neckband

With RS facing, smaller needles and C, pick up and k 72 (76, 76) sts evenly around neck edge. Work in k1, p1 rib for 7 rows. Bind off in rib.

### Embellishments

For fish tail on green fish, with D, cast on 6 sts. Work in St st for 4 rows. Dec 1 st each side on next row, then every other row once more. Cut yarn and draw through rem 2 sts. Attach as indicated on chart 2.

For braided tail on red fish, with crochet hook, ch 1"/2.5cm and knot one end. Make one each in B, D and F. Attach as indicated on chart 1.

For fish eyes, use French knots foll chart for placement and using D on chart 1 and B on chart 2.

For flag on boat, cut a piece of red felt foll chart 3 for pattern. Attach as indicated on one side.

For whale face, foll chart 5 and work chain st mouth with 3 strands B. Attach button for eye as indicated.

For drawstring, with crochet hook and B, ch approx 44"/111.5cm long and knot ends.

Sew right shoulder and neckband seam. Place markers 5 (5½, 6)"/12.5 (14, 15.5)cm down from shoulder seams on front and back for armholes. Sew top of sleeves between markers. Sew side and sleeve seams. Weave drawstring through eyelets at center front. Fold hem at lower edge of body to WS at turning ridge and sew in place.

### SHORTS

### BACK

With smaller needles and A, cast on 24 (26, 26) sts for left leg. Work in k2, p2 rib for ¾"/2cm, inc 1 (0, 1) on last row—25 (26, 27) sts. Change to larger needles and work in St st until piece measures 1¾ (2, 2½)"/4.5 (5, 6.5)cm from beg, end with a WS row. Place sts on a holder.

### Right leg

Work same as left leg but do not place sts on holder.

### Join legs

**Next row (RS)** Work sts of right leg, cast on 8 sts, work sts of left leg—58 (60, 62) sts. Cont on all sts until piece measures 8¾ (9¾, 10¾)"/22 (24.5, 27)cm from beg, end with a RS row. K next row on WS for turning ridge. Cont in St st for 1"/2.5cm more for waistband. Bind off.

### FRONT

Work as for back, beg with right leg.

### FINISHING

Block pieces to measurements. Sew side and inner leg seams. Fold waistband to WS at turning ridge leaving a small opening at center back for elastic and sew in place. Weave elastic through waistband casing and adjust to fit. Sew ends of elastic band tog. Sew rem opening closed.

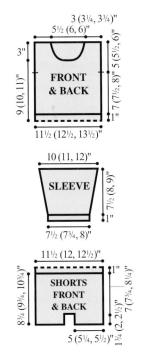

**Chart 1**

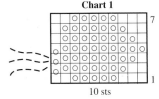

10 sts

**Chart 2**

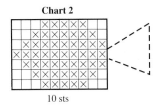

10 sts

**Chart 3**

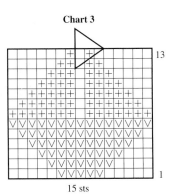

15 sts

**Color Key**

☐ Blue (A) or Stripe pat
⊙ Red (B)
✕ Green (D)
⊞ White (C)
▽ Yellow (F)
■ Charcoal (E)
• Blue (A)

**Chart 4**

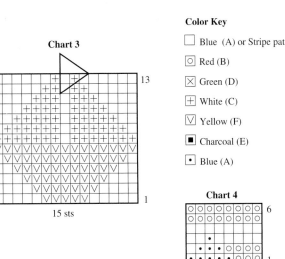

8 sts

**Chart 5**

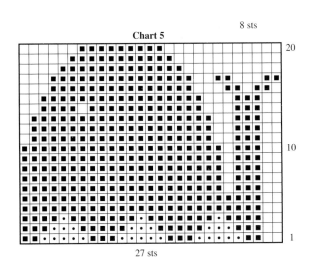

27 sts

# DOUBLE TROUBLE

*(Continued from page 44)*

## FRONT

Work as for back.

## SLEEVES

With A, cast on 32 sts. Work in St st for 2 rows.

### Beg chart 2

**Row 1 (RS)** Work first 4 sts of chart, work 12-st rep twice, work last 4 sts of chart. Cont as established through row 13. With A, bind off all sts.

## FINISHING

Block pieces to measurements. Sew one shoulder seam.

### Neckband

With RS facing and A, pick up and k 54 sts evenly around neck edge. Work in St st for 4 rows. Bind off loosely. Sew 2nd shoulder and neckband seam.

Sew top of sleeve to armholes. Sew side and sleeve seams.

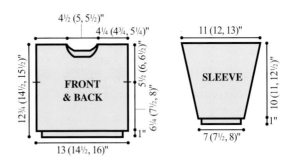

BOY'S SWEATER

TEDDY'S SWEATER AND HAT

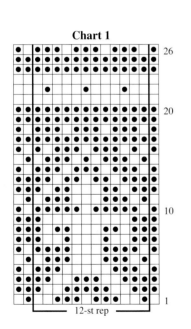

**Chart 1**

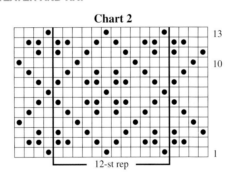

**Chart 2**

12-st rep

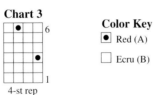

**Chart 3**

4-st rep

**Color Key**

● Red (A)

☐ Ecru (B)

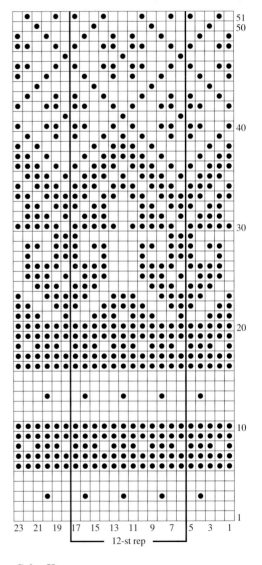

12-st rep

**Color Key**

● Blue (A)

☐ Ecru (B)

## BEAR NECESSITY

*(Continued from page 50)*

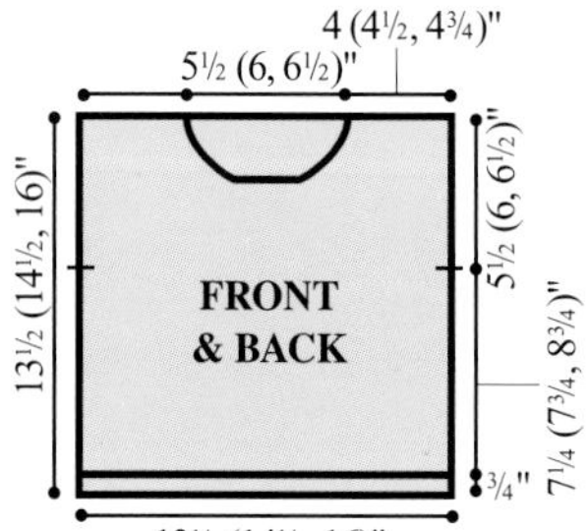
4 (4½, 4¾)"
5½ (6, 6½)"
13½ (14½, 16)"
FRONT & BACK
5½ (6, 6½)"
7¼ (7¾, 8¾)"
¾"
13½ (14½, 16)"

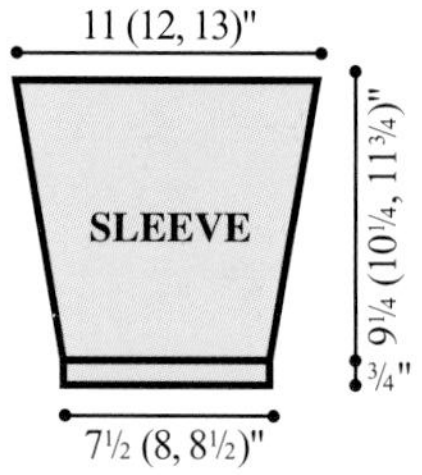
11 (12, 13)"
SLEEVE
9¼ (10¼, 11¾)"
¾"
7½ (8, 8½)"

**Chart 3**

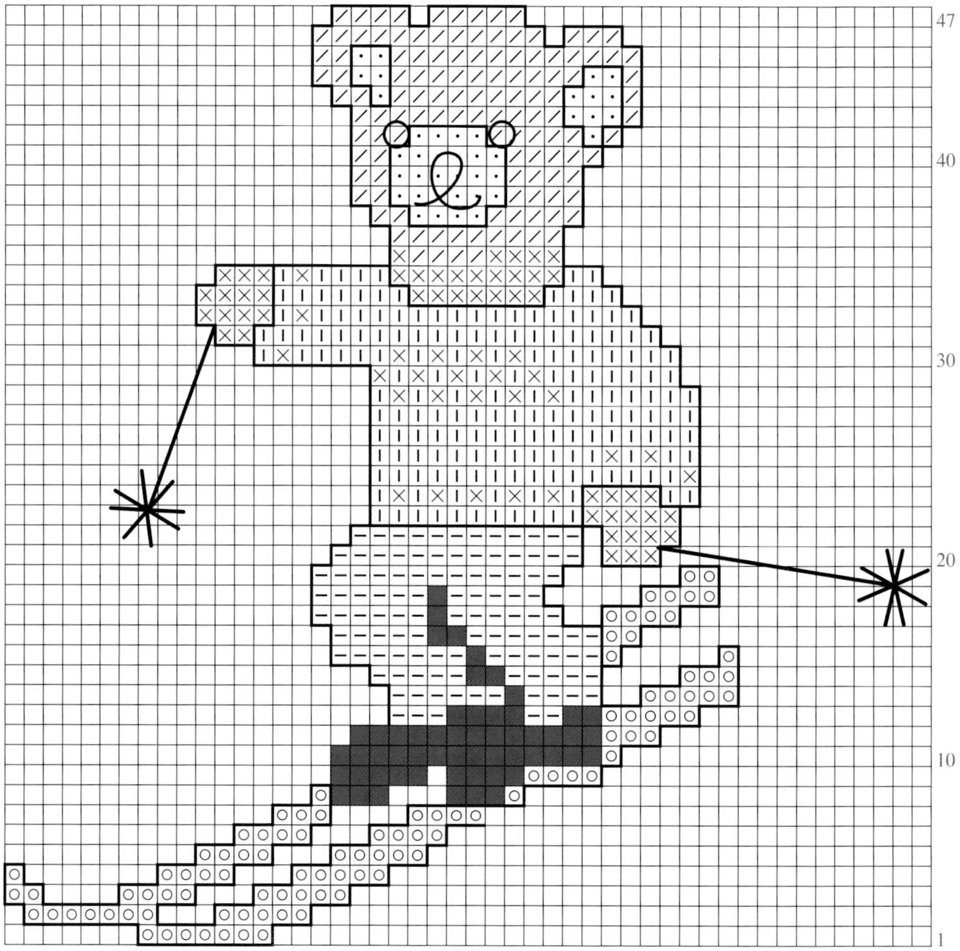
47
40
30
20
10
1

48 sts

**Color Key**

- Ecru (MC)
- Red (A)
- Brown (B)
- Green (C)
- Periwinkle (D)
- Tan (E)
- Charcoal (F)
- Black (G)

**Chart 1**

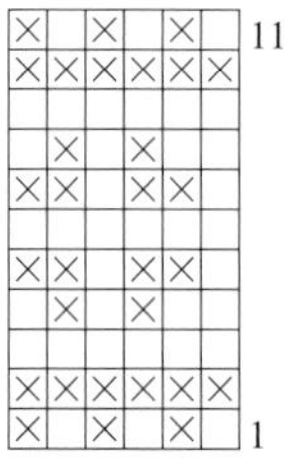
11
1

6- st rep

**Chart 2**

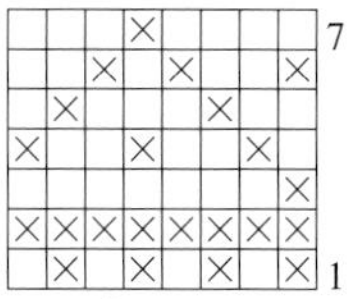
7
1

8- st rep

## MAD ABOUT BLUE

*(Continued from page 52)*

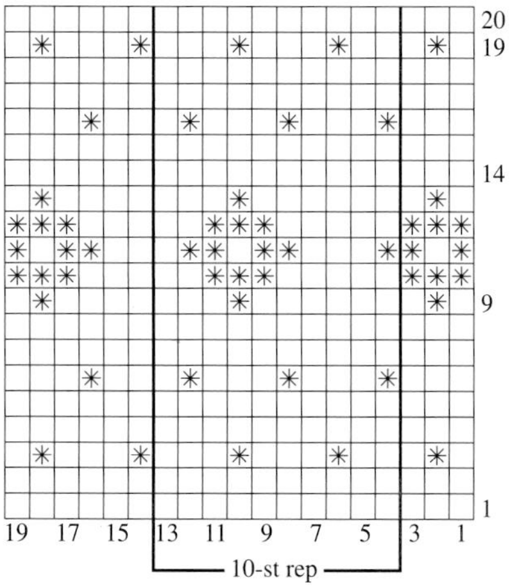
20
19
14
9
1
19 17 15 13 11 9 7 5 3 1
10-st rep

**Color Key**

- Blue (A)
- White (B)

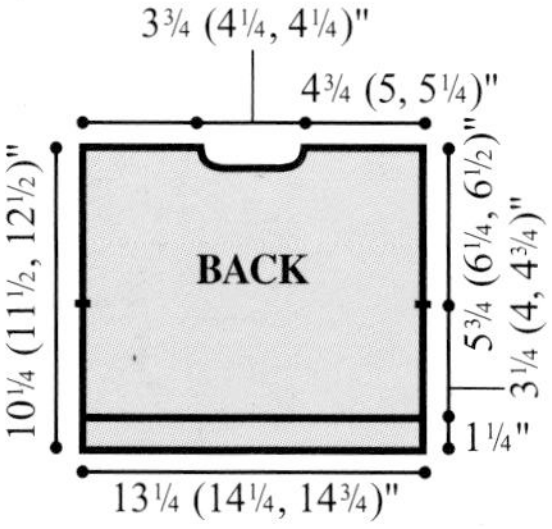
3¾ (4¼, 4¼)"
4¾ (5, 5¼)"
10¼ (11½, 12½)"
BACK
5¾ (6¼, 6½)"
3¼ (4, 4¾)"
1¼"
13¼ (14¼, 14¾)"

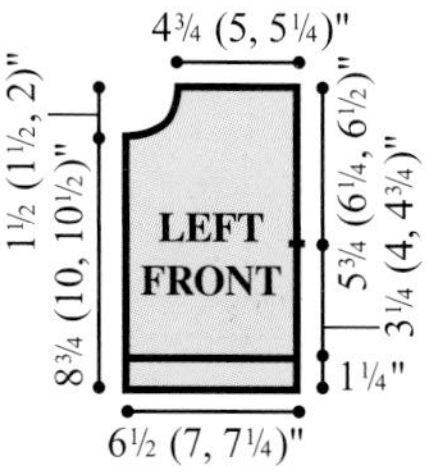
4¾ (5, 5¼)"
1½ (1½, 2)"
8¾ (10, 10½)"
LEFT FRONT
5¾ (6¼, 6½)"
3¼ (4, 4¾)"
1¼"
6½ (7, 7¼)"

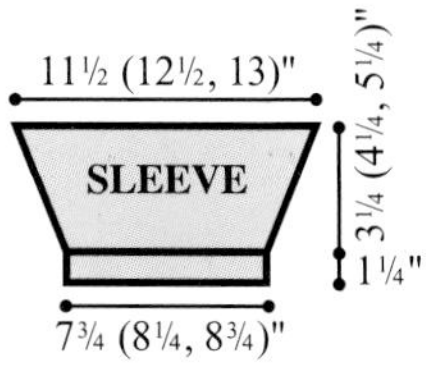
11½ (12½, 13)"
SLEEVE
3¼ (4¼, 5¼)"
1¼"
7¾ (8¼, 8¾)"

## BAA-BAA BABY

(Continued from page 54)

**CHART FOR PULLOVER AND BAG**

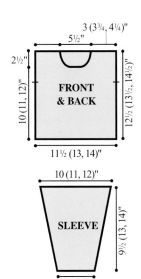

### Color Key

☐ Background color (MC)

🕸 French knot with Blue (A)

· Gold (C)

☒ White (B)

⟋ Chain st with Gold (D)

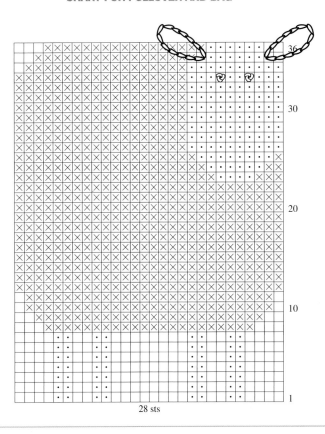

28 sts

## THE BIG TOP

(Continued from page 56)

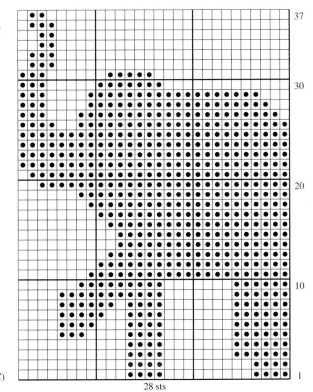

### Color Key

☐ Navy (MC)

● Chartreuse (CC)

28 sts

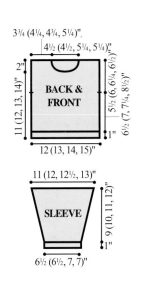

# Bits and Pieces

## LOOP DREAMS

*(Continued from page 76)*

to the left end all strands are ribbon, from the midpoint to the right end all strands are wool yarn. With a slip knot secure the ends of the A strands and fasten to a doorknob. Secure the ends of the B strands with a slip knot. Stand far enough away from the doorknob so that the piece hangs in midair and does not touch the ground.

Lay the B slipknot in your left palm and close your hand around it so that the slipknot hangs out by your thumb. Slip a pencil, knitting needle or any other long object in this and twirl it around while still holding the piece loosely in the left hand. Keep twirling until the strands begin to twist it around themselves. Cont twisting until the piece is quite taut and evenly twisted. Still holding B in your left hand, with your right hand pinch the twisted strands at the midpoint where A and B meet. Bring the ends of the cord tog by moving toward the doorknob, but do not let go of the middle of the yarn. Holding onto the ends of the yarn, now let go of the pinched midpoint of the twisted yarn—it will twist around itself. Determine the length of cord (approx 10"/ 25.5cm) and at that point fasten the yarn tog with a tight knot to keep the twisted cord from unraveling. Cut the excess yarn below the knot.

### Ribbon pompom

(make 3)

Wrap a strand of ribbon around three of your fingers ten times, cut the ribbon. Gently slip all of the ribbon off of your fingers and with a separate piece of ribbon tie the bundle together in the middle. With a needle and thread stab stitch the pompom in the middle several times to secure the loops securely. Stitch 1 pompom to one end of each of the twisted cords and stitch the other ends to the corners of the hat bottom. Stitch the third pompom to the very tip of the hat.

# Cradle Comforts

## TICKLED PINK

*(Continued from page 90)*

**Petal Square make 12**

Color A = Dark lilac
Color B = Dark pink
Color C = Pink
Color D = Lilac

## WHALE'S TALE

*(Continued from page 86)*

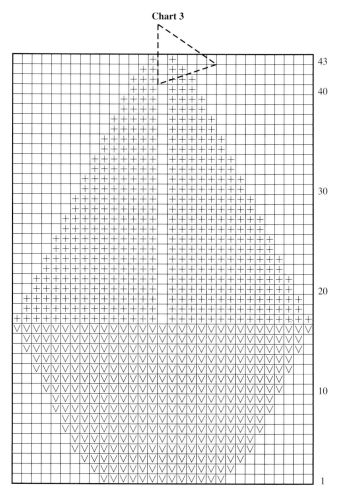

**Color Key**

- ☐ Blue (A) or Stripe pat
- ⊙ Red (B)
- ⊠ Green (D)
- ⊞ White (C)
- ⋁ Yellow (F)
- ■ Charcoal (E)
- ⊡ Blue (A)

*(Continued on page 86)*

**Color Key**

☐ Blue (A) or Stripe pat

⊡ Red (B)

☒ Green (D)

⊞ White (C)

⊻ Yellow (F)

■ Charcoal (E)

⊡ Blue (A)

**Chart 4**

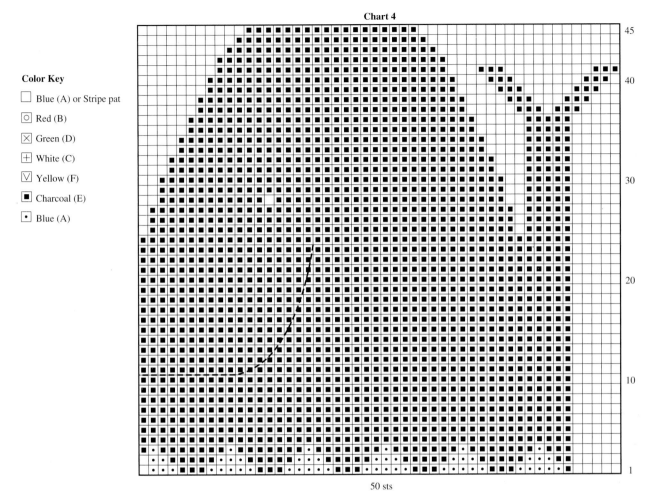

50 sts

**Chart 1**

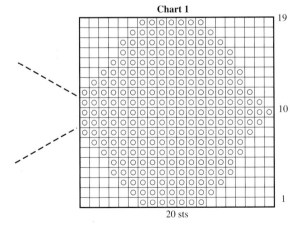

20 sts

**Chart 2**

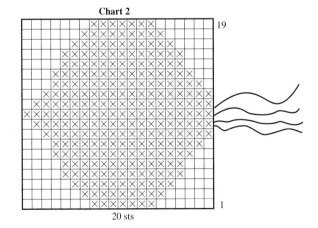

20 sts

# Cradle Comforts

## BARN DANCE

*(Continued from page 94)*

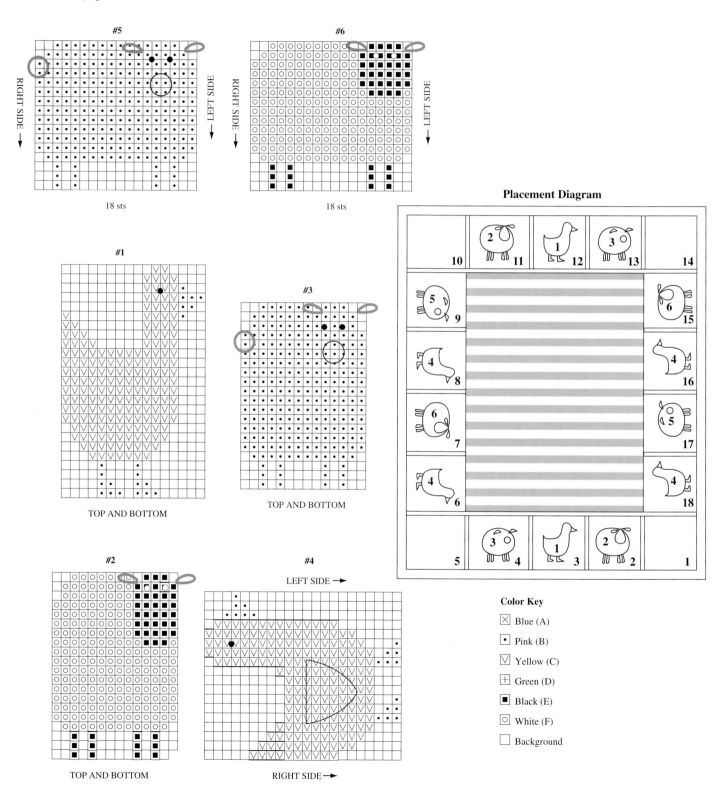

**#5**

RIGHT SIDE →

LEFT SIDE →

18 sts

**#6**

RIGHT SIDE →

LEFT SIDE →

18 sts

**#1**

TOP AND BOTTOM

**#3**

TOP AND BOTTOM

**#2**

TOP AND BOTTOM

**#4**

LEFT SIDE →

RIGHT SIDE →

**Placement Diagram**

**Color Key**

⊠ Blue (A)

• Pink (B)

∨ Yellow (C)

⊞ Green (D)

■ Black (E)

⊙ White (F)

☐ Background

# Toy Box

## RAINBOW TEDDY

*(Continued from page 98)*

Work 2-st Dec Row, p next row.] twice—28 sts. Work 4-st Dec Row on next 2 rows, bind off rem 20 sts.

### HEAD

With E, cast on 18 sts for left Side, pm, with F cast on 18 sts for right side. Working in colors as established, work 2 rows in St st.

**Row 3 (RS)** K across, inc in first and last st—20 sts.

**Rows 4 & 6** P across.

**Row 5** Work 4-st Inc Row—42 sts. **Row 7** Work 2-st Inc Row—44 sts.

**Row 8 (WS)** P across to 2 sts before marker, inc in both sts, sl marker, inc in next 2 sts, p across—48 sts.

**Row 9** K across.

**Row 10** Same as Row 8—52 sts. Rep Rows 7–10 twice more, then work Row 7 again—74 sts. Work 1 row even. Work Left and Right sides separately. (Gusset piece will fit into this area—see photo.)

### Left Side of Head

**(RS)** K across to marker, turn, place sts for right side of head on holder. Bind off 2 sts at beg of next row—35 sts. Dec 1 st at end of next 4 RS rows—31 sts. P across, then dec 1 st at each end of next 2 RS rows, then every row until there are 9 sts. Bind off rem sts.

### Right Side of Head

Sl sts from holder onto needle, ready to beg RS row. Cont with F, bind off 2 sts at beg of row—35 sts. Dec 1 st at beg of next 4 RS rows—31 sts. P across, then dec 1 st at each end of next 2 RS rows, then every row until there are 9 sts. Bind off rem sts.

### Head Gusset

Cast on 7 sts with G. Work in St st and inc 1 st each end of 5th row, and then every 6 rows until there are 21 sts. Work 5 rows even, then dec 1 st each end of next row, and then every 4 rows until 7 sts rem, then every other row twice—3 sts. Work 1 row even, then k1, k2 tog, turn. P2 tog, fasten off.

### Ears

(make 2)

Cast on 18 sts with A and work 8 rows in St st. Dec 1 st at each end of next 3 RS rows—12 sts, then every row 3 times—6 sts. Work 1 row even, break off A. Change to H, work 1 row even, then inc 1 st at each end of every row 3 times—12 sts, then next 3 RS rows—18 sts. Work 7 rows even. Bind off rem 7 sts. Work other ear the same using I & D.

### Arms

(make 2)

Cast on 2 sts with E, pm, cast on 2 sts with H. Working in colors as established, inc in each st across—8 sts.

**Next Row** [Work 2-st Inc Row, then 4-st Inc Row] 3 times—26 sts. Then work 2-st Inc Row on next 3 RS rows—32 sts. P next row.

**Next Row (RS)** [Inc in first st, work rest of row as 2-st Dec Row and inc in last st. P next row.] 5 times—32 sts. Work 6 rows even.

**Next Row** [Work 2-st Inc Row, then work 3 rows even] twice—36 sts. Change colors.

**Next Row (RS)** With G (in place of H) and F (in place of E), [k2 tog, work rest of row as 2-st Inc Row and dec at end of row. Work 3 rows even] 6 times—36 sts. Work 1 row even. Then work 4-st Dec Row 5 times, bind off rem 8 sts.

### Legs

(make 2)

Cast on 26 sts with C, pm, cast on 26 sts with B. Working in colors as established, work 2 rows in St st. Work 2-st Dec Row every row until 41 sts rem, work 1 row even. Work 2-st Dec Row on next 2 RS rows—38 sts, then every 4 rows twice—34 sts. Work 5 rows even, then work 4-st Inc Row—38 sts. Work 1 row even. Change colors: With A (in place of C) and I (in place of B), work 6 rows even, then work 4-st Inc Row—42. Work 7 rows even, then work 4-st Inc Row—46 sts. Work 5 rows even, then work 4-st Dec Row—42. Work 3 rows even, then work 4-st Dec Row, then every RS row twice—30 sts, then every row 5 times. Bind off rem 10 sts.

### Sole

(make 2)

Beg at Toe, cast on 4 sts with G, work 2 rows. Cast on 2 sts at beg of next 2 rows—8 sts. Then inc 1 st at each end of next 2 rows—12 sts. Work even for 14 rows. Dec 1 st at each end of next 2 RS rows, then every row 3 times—2 sts. K2 tog, fasten off.

### ASSEMBLY

Sew arm seams, leaving end open to stuff. Sew leg seams leaving bottom of foot open. Stuff, and then sew on sole. Sew gusset to right and left sides of head: cast-on edge of gusset goes where right and left sides separate at the nose. Sew back head seam leaving neck open for stuffing. Sew front and back body pieces tog, leaving open at bound-off edges for neck. Firmly stuff the head, body, and arms. Finish sewing arms shut. Sew head to body at neck. Fold ears in half and sew tog at side edges; sew to sides of head. Arms and legs can be sewn individually onto body, or by stitching each pair tog through body so that arms and legs move. Using black yarn, embroider face as shown in picture. Using Lazy-daisy, blanket stitch, feather stitch, and straight-stitch, embroider Teddy using photo as a guide.

## FUNNY BUNNY

*(Continued from page 100)*

and work to end. Working both sides at once with separate balls, work 3 rows even. Work dec row 2 as for back. Work 3 rows even. Work dec row 1 as for back. Work 1 row even. Work dec row 1. Work 3 rows even. Work dec row 2. Work 3 rows even. Work dec row 1. Work 1 row even. Bind off rem 6 sts each side. Sew center seam.

### FINISHING

Sew front to back and stuff. Sew on head. Sew on arms. For foot, work a running st around leg 1"/2.5cm above bottom of leg.

### SHORTALLS

With MC, cast on 48 sts for top side of leg and k 2 rows. Cont in St st for 10 rows. Bind off 2 sts at beg of next 2 rows. Dec 1 st each side every other row 4 times. Work even until piece measures 5"/13cm from beg. Dec 1 st each side every other row twice. Work 4 rows in garter st. Bind off. Work back side of leg in same way. Make a 2nd leg in same way.

### Straps (make 2)

With MC, cast on 3 sts and work in garter st for 7"/18cm. Bind off.

### FINISHING

Block pieces. With CC, whip st vertical stripes evenly spaced on pants foll photo. Sew front and back seams. Sew crotch seam. Sew straps and buttons to shortalls.

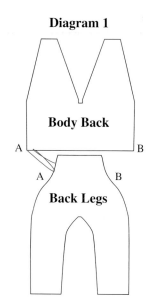

**Diagram 1**

Body Back

A      B

A      B

Back Legs

---

## TOBY TRICERATOP

*(Continued from page 104)*

**Next row** K3, M1, k1, M1, k4, M1, k1, M1, k3—16 sts. Work 3 rows even.

**Next row** K4, M1, k1, M1, k6, M1, k1, M1, k4—20 sts. Work 3 rows even.

**Next row** K5, M1, k1, M1, k8, M1, k1, M1, k5—24 sts. Work 3 rows even.

**Next row** K6, M1, k1, M1, k10, M1, k1, M1, k6—28 sts. Work 3 rows even. Cont in St st, inc 4 sts every 4th row as est 8 times more, then every other row 4 times—76 sts. Work 3 rows even.

### Shape top of tail

Bind off 6 sts at beg of next 10 rows—16 sts. Work 2 rows even.

### Shape gusset

Dec 1 st each side every other row 4 times, then every 4th row once—6 sts. Work 5 rows even. Inc 1 st each side every 4th row 6 times—18 sts. Inc 1 st each side every other row 7 times—32 sts. Work 3 rows even. Place sts on a holder.

### UPPER BODY

With RS facing and MC, pick up and k 37 sts evenly along top of left leg, k32 from gusset, then pick up and k37 sts evenly along right leg to top —106 sts. Work 3 rows St st, beg with a WS row.

**Next row** K35, k2tog, SKP, k28, k2tog, SKP, k35—102 sts. Work 3 rows even.

**Next row** K34, k2tog, SKP, k26, k2tog, SKP, k34—98 sts. Work 3 rows even.

**Next row** K33, k2tog, SKP, k24, k2tog, SKP, k33—94 sts. Work 3 rows even. Cont in St st, dec 4 sts every 4th row as est 5 times more—74 sts rem. Then dec 4 sts every other row 4 times—58 sts. Work 5 rows even.

### Shape neck

**Next row (RS)** K29, turn and cont on these 29 sts. Work 3 rows St st, AT SAME TIME, bind off 4 sts at beg of next 2 WS rows—21 sts.

**Next row** Knit.

**Next row (WS)** Bind off 4 sts, place marker (pm) for position of head frill, p to end—17 sts. Work 14 rows even. Dec 1 st at beg of next and every RS row until 13 sts rem, then dec 1 st from same edge every row 5 times—8 sts. Bind off. Join yarn to rem sts, bind off next 4 sts, k to end—25 sts. Work 1 row even. Work 3 rows St st, AT SAME TIME, bind off 4 sts at beg of every RS row twice—17 sts. Work 1 row, pm for head frill. Work 14 rows even. Dec 1 st at end of every RS row until 13 sts rem, then dec 1 st from same edge every row 5 times—8 sts. Bind off.

### HEAD

With MC, cast on 40 sts. Work 2 rows St st, pm at each end of first row for head frill position. Cast on 5 sts at beg of next 6 rows—70 sts. Work 20 rows even.

### Shape nose

**Next row** [K3tog] 5 times, k40, [k3tog] 5 times—50 sts.

**Next row** Purl.

**Next row** K10, [k3tog] 10 times, k10—30 sts.

**Next row** Purl. Bind off 8 sts at beg of next 2 rows—14 sts. Dec 1 st at each end of every row until 4 sts rem.

**Next row** P4tog. Fasten off.

### HEAD FRILL

*(make 2)*

With MC, cast on 12 sts. Work 2 rows St st. Cast on 4 sts at beg of next 2 rows, then 3 sts at beg of foll 2 rows—26 sts. Cast on 2 sts at beg of next 2 rows—30 sts. Inc 1 st at each side of next and every other row 3 times, then every 4th row once—38 sts. Work 3 rows even.

### Divide for head

**Next row** K13, turn and cont on these 13 sts. Dec 1 st at beg of next row, then at same edge in next 3 rows—9 sts. Work 1 row. Dec 1 st at end of next row—8 sts. Work 13 rows even, pm in last st of last row. Bind off. Join yarn to rem sts, bind off next 12 sts, k to end—13 sts. Dec 1

# TOBY TRICERATOP

*(Continued from page 136)*

st at end of next row, then at same edge in next 3 rows—9 sts. Work 1 row even. Dec 1 st at beg of next row—8 sts. Work 13 rows, pm in first st of last row. Bind off.

## Arms

(make 2)

With B, cast on 18 sts. P 1 row, pm in center of row.

**Next row** K into front and back loop of every st—36 sts.

**Next row** Purl. Break off B. With MC, work 14 rows St st, pm in center of 8th row.

**Next row** K4, [k2tog, k1] 10 times, k2—26 sts. Inc 1 st each side every other row 8 times—42 sts. Work 11 rows even.

## Shape top

Bind off 4 sts at beg of next 2 rows—34 sts. Dec 1 st each side every other row twice, then every row 5 times—20 sts. Bind off.

### HEAD FRILL BORDER

With RS facing, MC and beg at 2nd marker of one head frill piece, pick up and k 46 sts evenly down side edge to center of cast on edge, 1 st from center of cast on edge, then 46 sts to first marker—93 sts. **Row 1** Purl. **Row 2** Bind off 4 sts, *k5, bind off 3 sts, rep from * to last st. Place sts on holder.

## Horns

With RS facing and B, k across first set of 5 sts. **\*\*Next row** P5, turn. Next row K5, turn.

**Next row** P5 turn.

**Next row** SKP, k1, k2tog, turn.

**Next row** P3, turn.

**Next row** SKP. Pull yarn end through sts to secure.\*\*\* With RS facing, join B to next set of 5 sts. ** Rep between **'s 9 times, then work from ** to *** once (11 horns). Rep head frill border and horns on 2nd head frill piece.

## Head horns

(make 2)

With MC, cast on 18 sts. K 1 row on WS. With B,

work in St st, dec 1 st each side of 3rd row then every other row 7 times more—2 sts.

**Next row** K2tog. Pull yarn end through sts to secure.

### NOSE HORN

With MC, cast on 20 sts. K 1 row on WS. With B, work in St st, dec 1 st each side of 3rd row then every other row twice more—14 sts. Dec 1 st each side every row 6 times—2 sts.

**Next row** K2tog. Fasten off.

## Tail Bumps

(make 5)

With C, cast on 7 sts. Work 3 rows garter st, dec 1 st each side on 2nd and 3rd rows. Cast off rem 3 sts.

### FINISHING

With RS tog, backstitch 2 head frill pieces tog, leaving an opening at center of bound off edge. Turn head frill to RS. Stuff each horn, secure with a small stitch on inside. Stuff rem of head frill lightly and close opening. Join straight underseam of head. Place a point at each end of nose to end of underseam, then sew shaped edges to bound off sts at end of nose. Join bound off sts at top of neck shaping on upper body. Place head frill markers on head to head frill markers on neck shaping of upper body. Pin head frill between markers. Sew head frill in place, working through all 4 thicknesses. Sew rem of head in place to neck shaping. Join back seam of each leg. Sew soles of feet to base of legs, matching top of soles to toes of feet. Sew side edges of gusset to side edge of thighs. Sew rem edges of gusset to bound off sts of legs. Sew tail into tail opening. Join tail seam. Join back seam of toy, leaving an opening at base. Stuff toy and close opening. Join side edges of head and nose horns and stuff. Sew horns to top of head and nose as pictured. Sew cast on edge of tail bumps evenly spaced along tail seam. Join arm seams. Join

cast on edge of arms, matching marker at cast on edge to arm seam. Stuff arms. Sew a tight running st through both thicknesses of arm between marker at cast-on edge and 2nd marker. Sew tight running st halfway between first running sts and each edge of hand, to form 4 fingers. Sew top of arms to body. With D and stem st and satin st, embroider eyes to sides of head. Stem st nostrils to each side of nose and embroider mouth. Cut out different size circles from felt and glue to each thigh, tail and to front of head frill piece.

### SWEATER

## Back and front

With A, cast on 61 sts.

**Row 1** K2, *p1, k1; rep from *, k1.

**Row 2** K1, *p1, k1; rep from * to end. Rep rows 1 and 2 once, dec 1 st in center of last row—60 sts. Work in St st, dec 1 st each side, alternating dec rows between every 3rd and every 4th row until 48 sts rem, then dec 1 st every other row 8 times—32 sts. Work 1 row. Place sts on holder.

### SLEEVES

Cast on 35 sts. Work 4 rows rib as for back. Work in St st, inc at each end of 3rd and foll alt rows until there are 45 sts. Work 9 rows. Bind off.

## Neckband

With RS facing, k across 32 sts on front holder, 32 sts on back holder, inc 1 st in center—65 sts. Work 11 rows rib as for back, beg with a Row 2. Bind off loosely in rib.

### FINISHING

Backstitch shoulders tog, reversing seam on neckband for turn back. Fold neckband to RS and sew in place. Sew in sleeves. Sew side and sleeve seams.

## BARNYARD BUDDIES

*(Continued from page 106)*

**Rnd 3** Rep rnd 2—24 sc.

**Rnd 4** *Work 1 sc in next sc, 2 sc in next sc; rep from * around—36 sc. Join and fasten off. Sew nose to cover band as in photo.

### Embroidery

Using lazy daisy st and B, embroider toes foll chart. Using C, embroider eyes in French knots. Using B, embroider around eyes in chain st.

### Tail

With crochet hook and B, ch 27 firmly.

**Row 1** Sc in 2nd ch from hook and in each ch to end. Ch 1, turn.

**Row 2** Sc in each sc. Fasten off. Sew tail to back. Finish stuffing and sew final seam.

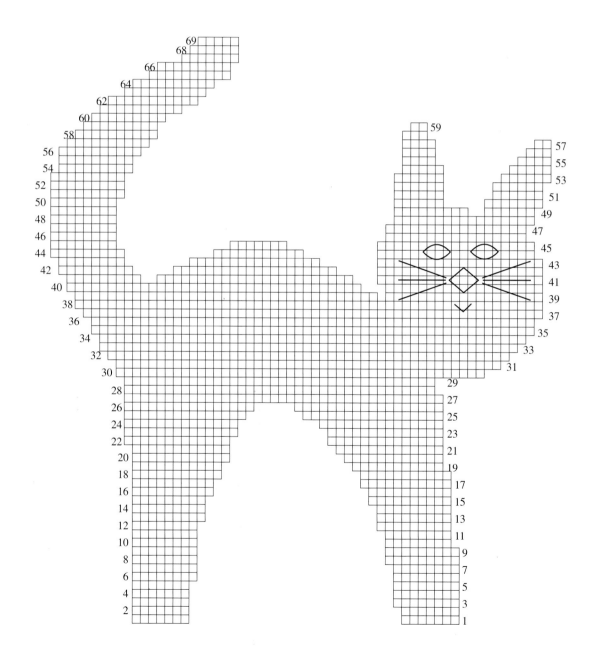

*(Continued from page 138)*

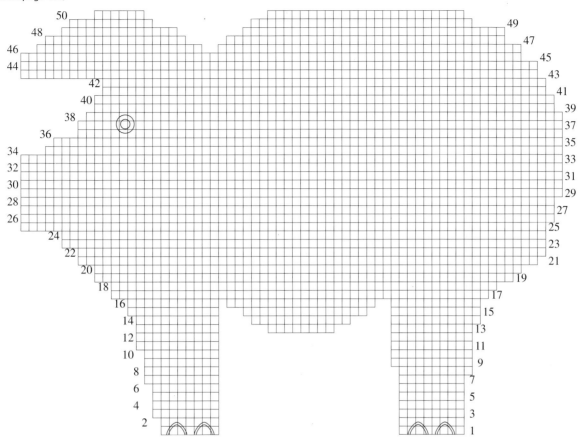

## BETSY BRACHIOSAURUS

*(Continued from page 108)*

to end—32 sts. Work 10 rows even. Bind off 4 sts at beg of next and every RS row 3 times—20 sts. **Next row (WS)** Cast on 2 sts, p to end—22 sts. **Next row** Bind off 4 sts, k to end—18 sts. **Next row** Cast on 4 sts, p to end—22 sts. Rep last 2 rows once, then first of these 2 rows once more. **Next row** Purl. Bind off 4 sts at beg of next and every RS row 3 times. Work 1 row even. Bind off rem 6 sts.

### TAIL

Cast on 10 sts as foll: 3 sts MC, 4 sts A, 3 sts MC. **Row 1** K3 MC, k4 A, k3 MC. [K 1 row, p 1 row matching colors] 3 times. **Row 7** (K2, M1, k1) MC, (k1, M1, k2, M1, k1) A, (k1, M1, k2) MC—14 sts. Work 5 rows even. **Row 13** (K3, M1, k1) MC, (k1, M1, k4, M1, k1) A, (k1, M1, k3) MC—18 sts. Work 5 rows even. **Row 19** [K3, (M1, k1)] twice MC, (k1, M1, k6, M1, k1) A, [(k1, M1)] twice, k3

MC—24 sts. Work 5 rows even. **Row 25** (K4, M1, k2, M1, k1) MC, (k1, M1, k8, M1, k1) A, (k1, M1, k2, M1, k4) MC—30 sts. Work 5 rows even. **Row 31** (K5, M1, k3, M1, k1) MC, (k1, M1, k10, M1, k1) A, (k1, M1, k3, M1, k5) MC—36 sts. Work 3 rows even. **Row 35** (K6, M1, k4, M1, k1) MC, (k1, M1, k12, M1, k1) A, (k1, M1, k4, M1, k6) MC—42 sts. Work 3 rows even. **Row 39** (K7, M1, k5, M1, k1) MC, (k1, M1, k14, M1, k1) A, (k1, M1, k5, M1, k7) MC—48 sts. Work 3 rows even. Cont to inc 6 sts every 4th row as est 6 more times—84 sts. Work 3 rows even. **Next row** (K2, M1, [K12, M1] twice, k1) MC, (K1, M1, k28, M1, k1) B, (k1, M1, [k12, M1] twice, k2) MC—92 sts. Work 3 rows even. Keeping colors correct, bind off 6 sts at beg of next 10 rows—32 sts.

### Shape gusset

**Next row** With B, k1, SKP, k to last 3 sts, k2tog, k1—30 sts. **Next row** Purl. **Next row** K1, SKP, k

to last 4 sts, k3tog, k1—26 sts. **Next row** Purl. Rep last 2 rows until 6 sts rem. Work 5 rows even. Cont in St st, inc 1 st each side every other row 15 times, then every 4th row twice—36 sts. Work 7 rows even. Place sts on holder.

### UPPER BODY

Using backstitch, sew gusset to front of thighs, matching top edges. Sew rem of gusset to bound off sts of legs. With MC, pick up and k 42 sts evenly across top of shaped edge of left leg, with A, k across 36 sts from holder, with MC, pick up and k 42 sts evenly across top of shaped edge of right leg—120 sts. Keeping colors correct, work 3 rows St st, beg with a purl row.

### Shape body

**Row 1** (K40, k2tog) MC, (SKP, k32, k2tog) A, (SKP, k40) MC—116 sts. Row 2 and all WS rows Purl.

## BETSY BRACHIOSAURUS

*(Continued from page 139)*

**Row 3** (K38, k3tog) MC, k34 A, (SK2P, k38) MC—112 sts. **Row 5** (K37, k2tog) MC, (SKP, k30, k2tog) A, (SKP, k37) MC—108 sts. **Row 7** (K35, k3tog) MC, k32 A, (SK2P, k35) MC—104 sts. **Row 9** (K34, k2tog) MC, (SKP, k28, k2tog) A, (SKP, k34) MC—100 sts. **Row 11** (K32, k3tog) MC, k30 A, (SK2P, k32) MC—96 sts. **Row 13** (K31, k2tog) MC, (SKP, k26, k2tog) A, (SKP, k31) MC—92 sts. **Row 15** (K29, k3tog) MC, k28 A, (SK2P, k29) MC—88 sts. Work 7 more rows, AT SAME TIME, cont to dec 4 sts every RS row as est, in colors as est. **Row 23** (SKP, k22, k2tog) MC, k24 A, (SKP, k22, k2tog) MC—72 sts. **Row 25** (K22, k2tog) MC, (SKP, k20, k2tog) A, (SKP, k22) MC—68 sts. **Row 27** (SKP, k19, k2tog) MC, k22 A, (SKP, k19, k2tog) MC—64 sts. **Row 29** (K19, k2tog) MC, (SKP, k18, k2tog) A, (SKP, k19) MC—60 sts. **Row 31** (SKP, k16, k2tog) MC, k20 A, (SKP, k16, k2tog) MC—56 sts. **Row 33** K18 MC, (SKP, k16, k2tog) A, k18 MC—54 sts. **Row 35** (SKP, k16) MC, k18 A, (k16, k2tog) MC—52 sts. Work 19 rows more, cont to dec 2 sts every other row as est in last 4 rows. **Row 55** (SKP, k11) MC, k8 A, (k11, k2tog) MC—32 sts. **Row 57** (SKP, k10) MC, k8 A, (k10, k2tog) MC—30 sts. **Row 59** (SKP, k9) MC, k8 A, (k9, k2tog) MC—28 sts. **Row 60** Purl. Work 10 rows even.

### Shape Neck

**Next row** K10 MC, turn and cont on these 10 sts. Dec 1 st at beg of next row, then dec 1 st at same edge every row 4 times more, then every other row 3 times—2 sts. **Next row** K2tog. Fasten off. Join A to rem sts, bind off next 8 sts, with MC, k to end—10 sts. With MC, cont on last 10 sts and complete to correspond with other side. Form neck into a tube, then stitch tog top of shaping where last st was fastened off at each side of neck.

### HEAD

With MC, cast on 4 sts, pick up and k 14 sts evenly along right side of neck to top of shaping, 14 sts down left side of neck, then cast on 4 sts—36 sts. **Next row** Purl. **Next row** Inc once in each of next 4 sts, k28, inc once in each of next 4 sts—44 sts. Work 11 rows St st, beg with a WS row. **Next row** K12, (k2tog) 10 times, k12—34 sts. **Next row** Purl. **Next row** K9, k2tog, [k3tog] 4 times, k2tog, k9—24 sts. Work 7 rows even. **Next row** [K2tog] 12 times—12 sts. **Next row** Purl. Break yarn, run thread through rem sts and draw tightly. Fasten off.

### ARMS

(make 2)

With B, cast on 18 sts. P 1 row. **Next row** K into front and back of every st—36 sts. **Next row** P15, pm in last st for end of finger, p18, pm in last st for end of finger, p3. With MC, work 7 rows St st. **Next row** P15, pm in last st for beg of finger, p18, pm in last st for beg of finger, p3. Work 2 rows. **Next row** K2 MC, k3 A, k31 MC. **Next row** P30 MC, p5 A, p1 MC. **Next row** K7 A, k29 MC. **Next row** P29 MC, p7 A. Rep last 2 rows twice more, then first of these 2 rows once. **Next row** (P2, [p2tog, p2] 6 times, p3) MC, p7 A—30 sts. Work 18 rows even keeping est colors.

### Shape shoulder

**Next row** With A, bind off 7 sts, with MC, k to end—23 sts. **Next row** With MC, purl. Dec 1 st at each side every other row twice, then every row 5 times—9 sts. Bind off.

### FINISHING

Join head under chin. Sew cast on sts of head to bound off sts of neck. Join back seam of legs. Sew soles to base of legs, matching top of soles to toes of legs. Join tail seam. Sew top edge of tail around tail opening. Join back neck seam for 6¼"/15cm from top of head shaping. Join rem of back seam, leaving an opening at base for stuffing. Stuff toy firmly and close opening. Join arm seams. Join cast-on edge of arms, matching markers. Stuff arms lightly. Sew a tight running st through both thicknesses of arm, between markers at cast-on edge and markers for beg of fingers. Sew running st as before, halfway between first running sts and each edge of hand, forming four fingers. Sew arms to each side of body, placing bound off sts of arms between markers on body. Using satin stitch and stem stitch and B and C, embroider eyes. Secure 6 ends of C with small sts to top of eyes and trim to ³⁄₈"/1cm lengths to form eyelashes. Cut circles from felt and glue to tail, back and neck.

*(Continued from page 114)*

Work 5 rows even.

Inc 1 st at each side of every row until there are 84 sts.

Work 4 rows even.

Tie a marker at each side of last row.

Dec 1 st at each side of every row until 78 sts rem.

Work 1 row even.

### Shape sides of face

**Next row** K2tog, k5, [k2tog] 13 times, k12, [k2tog] 13 times, k5, k2tog—50 sts.

Dec 1 st at each side of every row until 40 sts rem.

### Shape top

(right side of head)

**Next row** K2tog, k10, k2tog, turn.

Cont on these 12 sts for right side of head and dec 1 st at each side of every row until 2 sts rem. Work 1 row even. Bind off.

Sl next 12 sts onto holder and leave for gusset. With RS facing, join MC to rem 14 sts for left side of head.

**Next row** K2tog, k10, k2tog, turn.

Cont on these 12 sts for left side of head and dec 1 st at each side of every row until 2 sts rem. Work 1 row even. Bind off.

### Work gusset

With RS facing, join yarn to 12 sts from gusset holder and work 14 rows St st. Dec 1 st at each side of next row, then every 6th row until 6 sts rem, then every 4th row until 2 sts rem. Work 1 row even. Bind off.

Fold head piece in half and join front seam from neck edge to markers. Sew gusset evenly into position over top of head, ending at tip of nose (markers).

### Note

If you have purchased safety eyes that have a child proof backing, they will need to be attached to head now. Eyes that have shanks or holes can be attached on completion of bunny. Fill firmly and sew head to body, placing center seam of head to center front of body.

### Outer ear (make 2)

With smaller needles and MC, cast on 22 sts.

Work 12 rows St st. Dec 1 st at each side of next row, then every 12th row until 16 sts rem, then every 10th row once—14 sts. Work 7 rows even. Dec 1 st at beg only of next 8 rows—6 sts. Bind off.

### Inner ear

(make 2)

With smaller needles and A, cast on 19 sts. Work 12 rows in St st. Dec 1 st at each side of next row, then every 12th row until 13 sts rem, then every 10th row once—11 sts. Work 7 rows even. Dec 1 st at beg only of next 8 rows—3 sts. Bind off.

Join outer and inner ears tog in pairs, leaving base open. Oversew base edges tog and join side edges for 1½"/4cm. Sew ears on top of head, placing ears towards the back of the head.

### Legs

(make 2, beg at ankle)

With smaller needles and MC, cast on 14 sts. Work 2 rows St st.

**Row 3** K2, [inc in next st] 10 times, k2—24 sts. Work 3 rows.

**Row 7** K2, [inc in next st, k1] 10 times, k2—34 sts. Work 27 rows even.

### Shape top

**Next row** K2, [k2tog, k1] 10 times, k2—24 sts. Work 3 rows.

**Next row** K2, [k2tog] 10 times, k2—14 sts. Work 1 row even. Bind off.

### Feet (make 2, beg at sole)

With smaller needles and MC, cast on 4 sts. Work 2 rows St st.

**Next row** Inc in first st, knit to last st, inc in last st. Work 5 rows. Rep last 6 rows 3 times—12 sts. Work 8 rows even.

**Next row** K2tog, knit to last 2 sts, k2tog. Work 3 rows even. Rep last 4 rows twice—6 sts.

### Shape sides

Cast on 28 sts at beg of next 2 rows—62 sts. Work 4 rows in St st.

### Shape top

Dec 1 st at each side of every row 6 times—50 sts. Bind off 6 sts at beg of next 4 rows—26 sts. Work 2 rows even. Bind off.

Sew legs to lower side edges of body, leaving cast on edge open. Stuff leg, and stitch closed. Join top and front seam of each foot, then sew sole into position evenly. Pin feet in place, then sew securely.

### Arms (make 2, beg at top)

With smaller needles and MC, cast on 4 sts.

**Row 1** Inc in each st to last st, k1.

**Row 2** Purl.

Rep rows 1 and 2 once—13 sts.

**Row 5** K1, [inc in next st, k1] 6 times—19 sts.

**Row 6** Purl.

**Row 7** Inc in first st, knit to last 2 sts, inc in next st, k1.

Rep rows 6 and 7 four times—29 sts.

Place a marker at each end of last row to mark beg of arm seam.

Work 37 rows St st, dec 1 st in center of last row—28 sts.

**Next row** [K2, k2tog] 7 times—21 sts. Work 3 rows even.

**Next row** [K1, k2tog] 7 times—14 sts. Work 3 rows even.

**Next row** [K2tog] to end—7 sts.

Pull yarn through rem sts, draw up tightly and fasten off securely. Join seam from this point to markers.

Stuff firmly, then sew arms to body, inserting a little more filling before completing seam to keep firm.

### FINISHING

With MC make a 3"/7.5cm pompom and attach for tail (placing tail in a position where it will help bunny to stand.) With A embroider mouth and nose using satin stitch. Mark position of eyes. Insert needle through both marks then through the loop of one eye, take needle back through head again, through the other eye loop, and knot firmly so that eyes sink slightly into head. Darn in ends securely. If desired, brush bunny with a small stiff brush to bring up the pile of the mohair yarn.

### CARDIGAN

(Worked with B only)

*(Continued from page 141)*

### BACK

With smaller needles, cast on 53 sts.

**Row 1** K2, *p1, k1; rep from * to last st, k1.

**Row 2** K1, *p1, k1; rep from * to end.

Rep rows 1 and 2 twice, inc 1 st in center of last row (6 rows rib in all)—54 sts.

Change to larger needles. Work 6 rows in St st. Mark each end of last row for armholes. Work 28 rows in St st.

**Shape shoulders**

Bind off 7 sts at beg of next 2 rows, then 6 sts at beg of next 2 rows. Place rem 28 sts on holder.

### LEFT FRONT

With smaller needles, cast on 25 sts. Work 6 rows rib as for back, inc 1 st in center of last row—26 sts. Change to larger needles. Work 6 rows in St st.**

Mark end of last row for armhole.

Work 21 rows in St st.

**Shape neck**

**Next row (WS)** Bind off 7 sts, p to end—19 sts. Dec 1 st at neck edge every row 6 times—13 sts.

**Shoulder shaping**

Bind off 7 sts at beg of next row. P 1 row. Bind off rem 6 sts.

### RIGHT FRONT

Work as given for left front to **. Mark beg of last row for armhole. Work 20 rows in St st.

**Neck shaping**

**Next row** Bind off 7 sts, k to end—19 sts. Dec 1 st at neck edge of 2nd row, then every row 5 times—13 sts. K 1 row.

**Shoulder shaping**

Bind off 7 sts at beg of next row. K 1 row. Bind off rem 6 sts.

### SLEEVES

With smaller needles, cast on 37 sts. Work 6 rows rib as for back, inc 1 st in center of last row—38 sts. Change to larger needles. Work in St st, inc 1 st each side every 6th row until there are 44 sts. Work 5 rows even.

**Cap shaping**

Bind off 7 sts at beg of next 4 rows. Bind off rem 16 sts.

### FINISHING

Sew shoulder seams.

**Neckband**

With RS facing and smaller needles, pick up and k 13 sts evenly along right front neck, knit sts from back holder, dec 1 st in center, then pick up and k 13 sts evenly along left front—53 sts. Work 5 rows rib as for back, beg with row 2. Bind off loosely in rib.

**Left front band**

With RS facing and smaller needles, pick up and k 29 sts evenly along left front edge, including side edge of neckband.

Work 2 rows rib as for back, beg with row 2.

**Row 3 (WS)** Work 4 sts, *yo, work 2tog, work 8 sts; rep from * once, yo, work 2tog, work 3 sts—3 buttonholes.

Work 2 rows rib. Bind off loosely in rib.

**Right front band**

Work as for left front band, omitting buttonholes.

Sew sleeves between markers. Sew side and sleeve seams. Sew on buttons.

# Resources

## UNITED STATES RESOURCES

**Aurora Yarns**
PO Box 3068
Moss Beach, CA 94038

**Bernat®**
PO Box 40
Listowel, ON N4W 3H3
Canada
www.patonsyarns.com

**Berroco, Inc.**
P.O. Box 367
Uxbridge, MA 01569

**Classic Elite Yarns**
300 Jackson Street Bldg. #5
Lowell, MA 01852

**Cleckheaton**
distributed by Plymouth Yarn Co.

**Coats & Clark**
Attn: Consumer Service
PO Box 12229
Greenville, SC 29612-0229
(800) 648-1479
coatsandclark.com

**Colorado Yarns**
PO Box 217
Colorado Springs, CO 80903

**Filatura Di Crosa**
distributed by Tahki•Stacy Charles, Inc.

**Garnstudio**
distributed by Aurora Yarns

**Grignasco**
distributed by JCA, Inc.

**JCA, Inc.**
35 Scales Lane
Townsend, MA 01469

**Lang**
distributed by Berroco, Inc.

**Mission Falls**
distributed by Unique Kolours

**Mondial**
distributed by Skacel Collections

**Patons®**
P.O. Box 40
Listowel, ON N4W 3H3
Canada
patonsyarns.com

**Plymouth Yarn Co.**
PO Box 28
Bristol, PA 19007

**Reynolds**
distributed by JCA, Inc.

**Schoeller Esslinger**
distributed by Skacel Collections

**S.R. Kertzer, Ltd.**
105A Winges Road
Woodbridge, ON L4L 6C2
Canada
Tel: (800) 263-2354
www.kertzer.com

**Sesia**
distributed by Colorado Yarns

**Skacel Collections**
P.O. Box 88110
Seattle, WA 98138-2110

**Tahki Yarns**
distributed by Tahki•Stacy Charles, Inc.

**Tahki•Stacy Charles, Inc.**
8000 Cooper Ave., Bldg. 1
Glendale, NY 11385
Tel: (800) 338-YARN
tahki@worldnet.att.net

**Unger**
distributed by JCA, Inc.

**Unique Kolours**
1428 Oak Lane
Downingtown, PA 19335

**Wendy**
distributed by Berroco, Inc.

## CANADIAN RESOURCES

**Aurora Yarns**
PO Box 28553
Aurora, ON L4G 6S6

**Berroco, Inc.**
distributed by S. R. Kertzer, Ltd.

**Classic Elite Yarns**
distributed by S. R. Kertzer, Ltd.

**Diamond Yarn**
9697 St. Laurent
Montreal, PQ H3L 2N1 and
155 Martin Ross, Unit #3
Toronto, ON M3J 2L9

**Filatura Di Crosa**
distributed by Diamond Yarn

**Mission Falls**
P.O.Box 224
Consecon, ON K0K 1T0

**Patons®**
PO Box 40
Listowel, ON N4W 3H3

**S. R. Kertzer, Ltd.**
105A Winges Rd.
Woodbridge, ON L4L 6C2

We have made every effort to ensure the accuracy of the contents of this publication.
We are not responsible for any human or typographical errors.

# Acknowledgements

So many people contributed to the making of this book. First and foremost, we would like to thank the previous editors of *Family Circle Easy Knitting* magazine, including Nancy J. Thomas, Carla S. Scott, Margery Winter and Gay Bryant. We would also like to extend our gratitude to Barbara Winkler, Susan Kelliher Ungaro and Diane Lamphron from *Family Circle* for their vision and support. We would also like to acknowledge all the dedicated and knowledge-able past and present *Family Circle Easy Knitting* staff members for their support, dedication and hard work in bringing the best of knitting to their readers. Special recognition and appreciation goes to the tireless knitters and contributing technical experts, without whom the magazine would not be possible.

# Photo Credits

Scott Cameron
(pp. 105, 109)

Terrance Carney
(pp. 55, 69, 83, 85)

Jim Jordan
(pp. 17)

Brian Kraus
(pp. 23, 27, 31, 43, 67,
103, 107, 111, 115)

Rudy Molacek
(pp. 99)

Jose Santa
(pp. 89, 91, 93, 95)

Nick Vaccaro (pp. 57)

VNU Syndications
(pp. 9, 15, 19, 21, 29, 37, 39, 45,
47, 49, 51, 53, 61, 63, 65, 71, 101)

Marco Zambelli
(pp. 25, 33, 41, 73, 75, 77, 79, 87)